WORDLY WISE 3000®

THIRD EDITION

BOOK 5

Teacher's Resource Book

Systematic Academic Vocabulary Development

Kenneth Hodkinson | Sandra Adams

EDUCATORS PUBLISHING SERVICE
Cambridge and Toronto

Editorial Project Manager: Kate Moltz
Senior Editor: Will Tripp
Editor: Rachel Smith
Senior Designer: Deborah Rodman
Cover Design: Michelle Mohnkern

Printed in Benton Harbor, MI, in June 2016
ISBN 978-0-8388-7618-3

6 7 8 PPG 17 16

Contents

Program Preface and Components

We have to stop thinking of vocabulary as a supplemental activity. We must put it where it belongs, at the very core of the curriculum.

--Ken Hodkinson

Words are the tools we use to think, to express ideas and feelings, and to learn about the world. Because words are the very foundation of learning, improving students' vocabulary knowledge has become an educational priority. Student word knowledge is strongly linked with academic accomplishment because a rich vocabulary is essential to successful reading comprehension. Furthermore, the verbal sections of the high-stakes standardized tests used in most states are basically tests of vocabulary and reading comprehension.

Wordly Wise 3000®, Third Edition, has been designed to help students in kindergarten through grade 12 meet Common Core and state standards for vocabulary and reading comprehension. By using the lessons in the Student Book as well as the tools, strategies, and techniques provided in the Teacher's Resource Book, and supplementing both with the free website www.WordlyWise3000.com, you can make vocabulary development an effective part of your students' instruction.

Program Components

Kindergarten and Grade 1

Student Books

Teacher's Resource Books

Picture Cards

Concept Cards

Grades 2–12

Student Books

Teacher's Resource Books

- Teacher's Guide
- Student Book Answer Key
- Lesson Review Exercises and Answer Key
- Tests and Answer Key
- Word List

Audio Recordings

Test Generator

www.WordlyWise3000.com *(Free website)*

Wordly Wise 3000® Online

Teacher's Guide

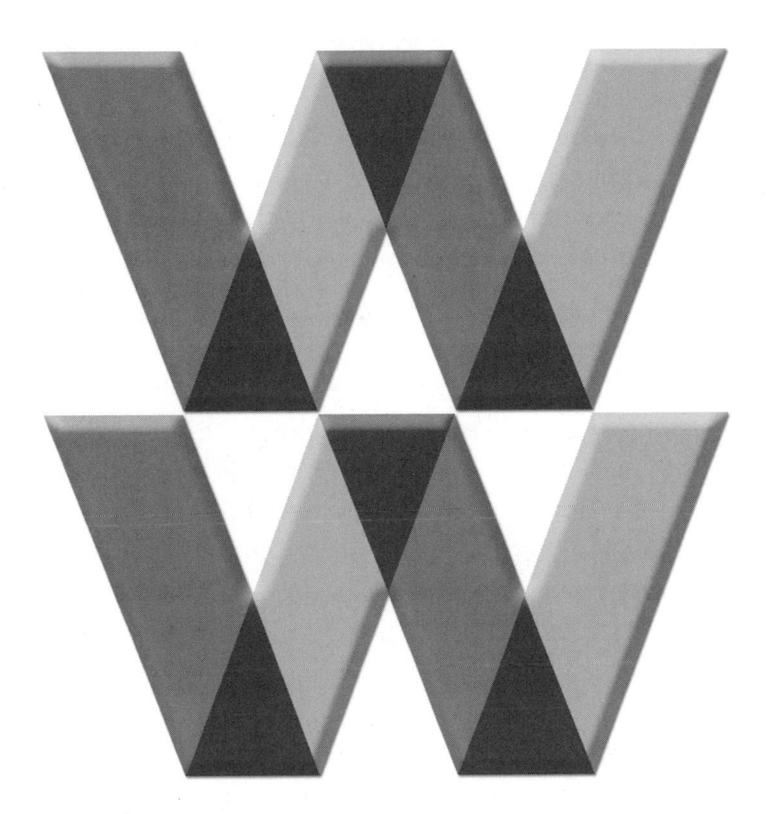

Chapter 1

What Is Good Vocabulary Development?

Why Teach Vocabulary?

Wordly Wise 3000®, Third Edition, focuses on improving students' vocabulary by furthering their understanding of new words and concepts. Studies have shown that reading comprehension and vocabulary knowledge are strongly correlated,[1] and researchers have found that word knowledge in primary school can predict how well students will be able to comprehend texts they read in high school.[2] Limited vocabulary prevents comprehension.

Poor readers often read less because reading is difficult and frustrating for them. This means they don't read enough to improve their vocabularies, which could help them comprehend more. This perpetuating cycle means that as students continue through middle school and high school, the gap between good and poor readers grows wider.

The good news is that direct vocabulary instruction can help break this cycle of failure. We know that good readers acquire much of their vocabulary indirectly—through wide independent reading. However, direct, explicit instruction can help students learn enough words to become better readers and thus acquire even more words.

Direct vocabulary instruction is useful for students at all levels, but it is particularly useful for beginning students who have a limited vocabulary and little exposure to incidental vocabulary learning outside of school. We know that students come to school with vastly different vocabularies. Some will know thousands more word meanings than others. This occurs in part because of the differences in the number of words students are exposed to in their homes and communities. Students who come from homes where spoken and written vocabularies are limited will know fewer words than students from homes where exposure to a wide range of vocabulary is common. However, arriving in class with a small vocabulary does not predict failure—it only highlights the need for direct vocabulary instruction in the school. As one researcher put it, "If we are serious about 'increasing standards' and bringing a greater proportion of schoolchildren to high levels of academic accomplishment, we cannot continue to leave vocabulary development to parents, chance, and highly motivated reading."[3]

Studies have shown that the key to increasing vocabulary is exposure to new words, not an innate ability to learn from context.[4] Experts emphasize that vocabulary development is an attainable goal. If given the systematic opportunity to learn new words via effective direct instruction, most students can acquire vocabulary at rates that will improve their comprehension. This enables them to read increasingly challenging texts with fluency and improves their chances for success in school and beyond.

On average, students learn about 3,000 words per year, all told, or six to eight words per day—a remarkable achievement! If students are taught new words at a rate of eight to ten words per week for 37 to 50 weeks, about 300 to 500 words per year can be taught through direct instruction.[5] This still leaves a large portion of words to be learned incidentally. Although the percentage of words learned through direct instruction may seem small, it is significant. Stahl has pointed out that for students at the lower end of the vocabulary range, who learn perhaps 1,000 words a year, a gain of 300 words equals a 30 percent increase, and that for average students, a gain of even 10 percent is educationally significant—especially if it is repeated year after year.[6] Experts agree that a combination of direct instruction of word meanings, discussions about words and word parts, and encouragement of wide reading is the best way to help students develop vocabulary.

What Words Should Be Taught?

Equally important to the sheer number of words students learn is the kinds of words they learn. Regardless of how many words students know upon entering school, most of them will have sufficient vocabulary for everyday tasks such as playing with peers and watching television. These are the words Beck and her colleagues identify as Tier One words in their Three-tier hierarchy.[7] But to do well in school, they must know the language of school—the words they find in books, from novels to textbooks, in online articles, and on tests. School, or academic, language—Beck's Tier Two words—also includes general instructional language, such as *summarize* and *develop,* as well as the words used in outside reading, and those that are liable to have utility across various fields of study. Tier Two words are those that are likely to have the most direct impact on students' academic lives. In addition to this general academic language, students need content-area specific language as well. These are Tier Three words, and they are taught most effectively within the context of a content area. As Stahl and Nagy say, "The language of conversation, and of television, simply is not adequate preparation for the language that students will encounter in their texts."[8]

Wordly Wise 3000 is designed to teach primarily Tier Two words with a healthy smattering of Tier Three words. A companion EPS/School Specialty Literacy and Intervention program devoted solely to content-area vocabulary in Science and Social Studies is *Wordly Wise Science and Social Studies*™. This program, featuring Tier Three words, serves as an excellent complement to *Wordly Wise 3000* as part of a total vocabulary development curriculum. It is available for grades 4–8 and is an online program that can be used independently, as a classroom supplement, or both. Learn more about *Wordly Wise Science and Social Studies* at epsbooks.com.

What Should Direct Instruction Include?

What is the best way to teach students to acquire words? Best practice indicates that effective vocabulary instruction should include:

- both definitional and contextual information about a word;
- multiple exposures to the word in different contexts;
- encouragement of students' active participation in their own word learning.[9]

Definition and Context

Traditionally, vocabulary instruction has not been instruction at all, but has focused on having students look up word meanings and memorize them. This approach provides only superficial and short-term learning of words. Students who simply memorize definitions frequently have trouble applying the information and often make mistakes about the meanings.[10]

To know a word, students need to see it in context and learn how its meaning relates to the words around it. An approach that includes definitions as well as context can generate a full and flexible knowledge of word meanings. When students are given several sentences that use a word in different ways, they begin to see how a word's meaning can change and shift depending on its context. For example, consider the changes in the word *got* as it appears in the following sentences:

Joseph got a cold.

Joseph got rich.

Joseph got a note from Krishna.

Krishna got in trouble.

Although in most of these examples, *got* conveys the idea of receiving, the meaning is slightly different in each one. Based on the concept that students need to see words in different contexts in order to learn them, each lesson provides definitions of the vocabulary words—some with multiple meanings—and several examples of their use in context, as well as exercises in which they can be applied.

Context helps students make connections between and among words, and these connections can deepen understanding. For example, students may have difficulty with the meaning of the word *symbol* (Book 4, Lesson 15), but if they learn it in context of a passage about the bald eagle, America's symbol, they will more easily understand its meaning. What's more, they will begin to develop a deeper knowledge of the word as they think about and discuss other symbols.

Multiple Exposures

Students benefit from interacting with a word several times. Word meanings are accumulated gradually. A word that is encountered once has about a 10 percent chance of being learned from context.[11] When students see a word repeatedly, they gather more and more information about it until they acquire an idea of what it means. Dale and O'Rourke have summarized the four stages of word knowledge:

1. I never saw it before.
2. I've heard of it, but I don't know what it means.
3. I recognize it in context—it has something to do with . . .
4. I know it.[12]

The more exposure students have to a word, the more likely it is that they will know it well and deeply. Good vocabulary instruction builds repetition into the learning process so that students can learn more words more quickly. Each lesson in *Wordly Wise 3000* asks students to use and apply several of the lesson's words in different and increasingly sophisticated contexts as they complete the exercises.

Encouraging Active Participation

Students remember words better when they connect new meanings to knowledge they already have. This type of active processing occurs when students work with words in some of the following ways: producing antonyms and synonyms; rewriting definitions; identifying examples and non-examples of the word; using more than one new word in a sentence; creating sentences that contain the word.[13]

Each activity reinforces definitional or contextual information about the word and gives students a chance to own the word for themselves. Group discussion of word meanings requires active participation and encourages deep and flexible knowledge of words.

How, When, and Where to Use *Wordly Wise 3000*

Wordly Wise 3000 is designed for maximum flexibility. The lessons can be used in different settings (in class, at home, in one-on-one tutoring sessions), at different frequencies (once a week, three times a week, every day), and in varied sequences (lessons can be followed in numerical order or used individually). Teachers have told us they use *Wordly Wise 3000* in several ways:

- as in-class activities
- as homework
- as independent study
- as preparation for standardized tests or spelling bees

In general, we recommend more in-class direct instruction at the primary grades, more student-centered guidance and coaching as students proceed through the upper elementary grades and middle school, and more independent work in high school. Of course, the way you use *Wordly Wise 3000* depends on the needs of your students and on your classroom situation. We recognize that many teachers have students with different reading levels in their classrooms. The *Wordly Wise 3000* series can help a teacher accommodate these differences. By choosing the appropriate level of the *Wordly Wise 3000* books for particular students, teachers can ensure that their advanced students stay challenged and their struggling students have material that suits their learning level.

The FREE www.WordlyWise3000.com website adds another layer of flexibility to using the program. Students can access the site anywhere an Internet connection is available. The site has many features that make it ideal for all students:

- **Full Audio Word Lists** match each book's Word Lists, presenting the word, its part of speech, its definition, and a sample sentence. All of these are read aloud to students.
- **A Quick Check Question** Once students have read an entry, they are presented with a question that allows them to see right away whether or not they understood the word's meaning.
- **MP3 Downloadable Files** The lesson words, parts of speech, definitions, and sample sentences are downloadable to any MP3 device, allowing students to store them for study anywhere—at home, on the school bus—to make the best use of study time.
- **Games** A series of interactive games is available following every fourth lesson. This cumulative structure provides review opportunities for students in an engaging and dynamic way.

This valuable free resource is ideal for all students, but may be especially helpful for struggling students and for English language learners.

Audio support can help students who struggle with pronunciation, sound-symbol match, and fluency. Audio is presented by a human voice, not an artificial sounding text-to-speech voice.

The website www.WordlyWise3000.com provides exposure to words at a variety of grade levels that meet students exactly where they need to be.

Teacher Materials

The www.WordlyWise3000.com website also provides a number of downloadable graphic organizers that teachers can use with students who need more practice with the words in *Wordly Wise 3000*.

Sample Teaching Plans

Our research shows that about half of the teachers working with *Wordly Wise 3000* teach vocabulary two or three times per week. About a third teach vocabulary almost every day, and ten percent teach vocabulary once a week. (Percentages do not add up to 100 because some teachers did not answer this question or chose "other" in our survey.) The *Wordly Wise 3000* series can accommodate these individual schedules. Here are some typical plans.

Once-a-Week Teaching Plan

If you are able to devote only one class per week to vocabulary, it is best to use that time to help students become familiar enough with the new words that they can complete the exercises outside of class on their own. Such a teaching plan might look like this:

Vocabulary Day

As a class, go over the Word List thoroughly. Have students read the definitions and sample sentences aloud. Ask students to use the words in sentences of their own. Use queries, illustrations, pantomimes, and graphic organizers to encourage discussion of what a word means and how it differs from related words. Make a Word Wizard chart (see page xvi) that contains all the week's vocabulary words and display it in the classroom. Ask students to be on the lookout for the words outside the classroom. When they encounter one of them, they can add their names to the chart with their examples of how each word was used. Assign all or a selection of the exercises in the lesson as homework for the following week. Remind students to use the free www.WordlyWise3000.com website to study and practice.

Three-Days-a-Week Teaching Plan

Teachers who can devote three days a week to vocabulary instruction should be able to complete one lesson per week, with students doing most of the exercises in the Student Book and some of the activities and enrichments suggested in this Teacher's Guide. Such a teaching plan might look like this:

Day 1

Introduce the Word List to the class and facilitate discussion about each item. Complete the Finding Meanings exercise as a group. Assign the Just the Right Word and Applying Meanings exercises as homework to be ready by the next vocabulary class day.

Day 2

Refresh the students' memories about the words in the lesson by asking volunteers to briefly define each one. Review the homework as a group, having students explain why one answer is correct and the others wrong. Have a student or students read the Passage aloud. Assign the Word Study and Passage questions as homework to be ready by the next vocabulary class day.

Day 3
Review the homework as a group, again having the class discuss what makes the correct answer correct. Reinforce the students' new knowledge by having them pick five words from the list to use in a short story or essay on any topic. Remind students to use the free website to study their words at any time.

Five-Days-a-Week Teaching Plan
Teachers who teach vocabulary every day should be able to complete one lesson per week, with students doing all the exercises in the Student Book, many of the activities and enrichments suggested in this Teacher's Guide, and using the website. Such a teaching plan might look like this:

Day 1
Introduce the Word List to the class and facilitate discussion about each item. Use queries, illustrations, pantomimes, and graphic organizers to encourage discussion of what a word means and what it doesn't mean. Assign the Finding Meanings exercise as homework to be ready by the next class day.

Day 2
Review the homework as a group, having students explain why one answer is correct and the others wrong. Have the students complete the Just the Right Word exercise in small groups, then discuss the answers as a class.

Day 3
Complete the Applying Meanings and Word Study exercises by calling on students one at a time. Query the class to gauge their understanding, and solicit explanations from other class members to clarify meanings.

Day 4
Have the students read the Passage and answer the questions that follow on their own. Discuss the answers as a class.

Day 5
Have the students demonstrate their mastery of the new words by paraphrasing—rewriting definitions for the words—and by using the words in their own sentences or stories.

Remind students to use the free website to study their words at any time.

Placing Your Students in *Wordly Wise 3000*

The Student Books in *Wordly Wise 3000* correspond to grade levels. While Book 5 corresponds to grade 5, many teachers report using a variety of levels with their classes, either for students who struggle with on-level material or for more challenging material for their ablest students. We recommend that, in general, you begin a student in the *Wordly Wise 3000* book corresponding with his or her nominal grade.

Wordly Wise 3000 has a new feature to help you place students at the best level for them. All the reading passages have been assigned measures using The Lexile Framework® for Reading. See the chart below for the Lexile® ranges covered in each Student Book. If you know students' Lexile measures, it's a simple matter of matching them to the *Wordly Wise 3000* book. If you do not know your students' Lexile measures, you may want to visit the MetaMetrics®, Inc. website at www.MetaMetricsInc.com.

Passage Lexile Ranges

Book	Range
2	300L–500L
3	500L–700L
4	650L–850L
5	750L–950L
6	850L–1050L
7	950L–1075L
8	1000L–1110L

Struggling Readers and English Language Learners

Struggling readers and those learning English face a challenge in learning vocabulary. Since vocabulary is key to comprehension, students who don't understand the meaning of words they read are at a disadvantage. Yet, in order to learn those words, they need to read and interact with them. This cycle of frustration is all too common as students progress through elementary and middle school. Breaking this cycle is a challenge for their teachers as well. The free website www.WordlyWise3000.com can provide a dedicated tutor for these students, since it provides pronunciation and models fluent reading. For these students, *Wordly Wise 3000® Online,* with its rich scaffolding, might also provide an excellent solution. See pages xxxiv–xxxvi for a description.

Chapter 2

Strategies and Techniques for Teaching Vocabulary

Effective vocabulary development is a multifaceted process requiring a combination of direct instruction, discussion, and active encouragement of independent learning strategies. On their own and in the classroom, students draw on a variety of methods to learn the thousands of words they acquire each year. This part of the Guide will discuss the following general strategies and specific techniques to keep in mind as you teach vocabulary:

- encouraging wide reading
- emphasizing learning from context
- using roots, prefixes, and suffixes
- using graphic organizers such as semantic maps, concept of definition maps, semantic feature analysis, and Venn diagrams
- extending instruction through reading aloud and discussion

These approaches will enhance your vocabulary curriculum and can be used to supplement the direct instruction that *Wordly Wise 3000* provides.

Encourage Wide Reading

Getting your students to read more may be the most valuable thing you can do to improve their vocabulary. Although direct instruction plays a crucial part in vocabulary growth, most of the words your students learn will be acquired through incidental learning, as they read on their own. The average student learns about 3,000 words a year. Although direct instruction plays a crucial part in vocabulary growth, evidence shows that wide reading is the main avenue for student word acquisition. Researchers present this scenario to demonstrate the effectiveness of wide reading:[14]

- If, over a school year, a fifth-grader reads for an hour each day, five days a week, in and out of school at a conservative rate of 150 words per minute, the student will encounter 2,250,000 words in the course of reading.
- If 2 to 5 percent of the words the student encounters are unknown words, he or she will encounter from 45,000 to 112,500 new words.
- We know that students learn between 5 and 10 percent of previously unknown words from a single reading. Using the lower number given above for unknown words encountered during the reading program, we see that a student would learn at least 2,250 new words from context each year.

This estimate suggests that incidental learning is critical to vocabulary development. Again, the more students read, the more word meanings they will know and the more likely they will be to read with both pleasure and comprehension.

To be beneficial, wide reading should include texts with varied levels of difficulty. Students reading at or below their current levels will not dramatically increase their vocabulary. However, when students read texts that consist of too many unknown words, they become frustrated. In order to get the most out of incidental learning, suggest some books to be read for fun and others for a challenge.

Motivating students to read can be a difficult task. Here are a few suggestions for making reading appealing to students at all ability levels:

- Devote some class time to independent silent reading. Instituting and modeling this practice may be particularly helpful for students who have never done extensive reading for pleasure and for those who do not see reading for pleasure in their homes.
- Make a variety of books available in class and recommend books for students to find in the library and to read outside of class. You might want to provide lists of books you think students would enjoy, based on an informal survey of their interests.
- Promote social interactions related to reading. Set up a Book Club or at least a time for regular discussions of books. This will motivate students to read more and help them understand their reading better.
- Model the importance of reading by sharing information about your own reading. When students have silent reading time, read a book of your own to show that reading is a valuable activity that you enjoy, too.

These strategies will have long-term benefits for your students. Wide reading is a key component to vocabulary development, but as with much important learning, its effects are cumulative rather than immediate.

Emphasize Learning from Context

Most of the words acquired through incidental reading are learned through context. Students learn from context by making connections between a new word and the text in which it appears. As noted earlier in this Guide, students learn words through repeated exposures, gaining more comprehension of a word's meanings and functions by seeing it several times in different contexts.

Experts debate the effectiveness of teaching students how to use context clues. While some studies show that teaching students how to identify and use context clues is an effective technique for increasing vocabulary,[15] other research suggests that learning words from context is an innate skill that all readers use. Kuhn and Stahl have found that children of all abilities learn at the same rate from context; that is, advanced readers are no more efficient at learning from context than less advanced readers—the advanced readers simply read more.[16] All experts, however, stress that it is crucial to make students aware of the importance of using context clues as an essential tool in word acquisition.

Here are some techniques for enhancing students' awareness of the importance of context clues:[17]

- Model basic strategies for using context clues, when working with *Wordly Wise 3000* or reading other texts.
- Provide explanations of how, when, and why to use context to figure out word meanings.
- Provide guided practice, including Think-Alouds, in using context.
- Remind students to apply the skill when reading.

You can also use activities such as a Word Wizard chart (developed by Beck et al.) to make students aware of learning words in context.[18] As you discuss unfamiliar words in class, you can add them to the chart. If a student comes across one of these words either in print or orally, notes where this happened, and discusses the context, his or her name goes up on the chart. You can provide students with periodic rewards for contributing many words to the chart.

Word Wizard Chart

Name	Word	Location
Tyrese	valiant	novel
Ilana	fortunate	TV
Eric	instant	sign
Olivia	replace	video game

Another way to emphasize the importance of learning from context is to have students rate their knowledge of a new word by using a checklist:

Knowledge Rating Checklist
How much do I know about these words?

	Can define	Have seen/heard	Don't know
conclude		✓	
elder	✓		
forlorn			✓
hearty		✓	
inhale	✓		
merit	✓		
stingy	✓		
summon		✓	
valiant			✓

These checklists can also be used in group activities in class. You may also want to have students keep these checklists together in a notebook along with a running list of words they come across that intrigue or interest them. Encouraging a general awareness of words as fun and interesting in themselves will help students pursue their own vocabulary development.

Using context is an important skill that students will employ frequently. However, in learning when to use context clues, students also need to know when not to use this strategy. Since many texts do not signal the meanings of words explicitly, using context is not always the best way to derive the meanings of new words.

Part Smart: Use Roots, Prefixes, and Suffixes

Experts have noted that the upper elementary grades are a good time to start teaching students how to use word parts to figure out the meanings of words.[19] Information from roots, prefixes, and suffixes can help students learn and remember words. Using word parts can be a particularly useful strategy in reading content-area texts. For example, science texts often include words that use the same word parts, such as *bio-* in *biosphere, biology, biodegradable, bioluminescence,* and *biochemical.* Knowing that *bio* means "life" can help students recognize these words in context and add to their comprehension of these words. This particular root will also help students learn words across content areas. For example, students will encounter words such as *biography* as they study literature.

You might begin to teach word-part strategy by telling students that words can be composed of affixes—prefixes and suffixes—and roots. Learning to break words into affixes and roots will make some long words more manageable for students who may be intimidated by the length of words such as *interdependent.* Modeling how to break words into parts may be necessary. To do this, teach students to cover prefixes such as *inter-* in the word *interdependent,* and see if they recognize the rest of the word. Then have them cover the suffix *-ent,* leaving *depend.*[20] Further modeling and practice with adding and removing prefixes and suffixes such as *un-* and *-able* will give students facility with breaking words down into parts. In teaching word parts, make sure to stress how the parts function to affect word meaning. You may want to point out that prefixes such as *un-, super-, anti-, mis-,* and *sub-* change the meanings of the roots they precede in predictable ways. Since prefix definitions are quite consistent, you may want to supply them, as shown in the following table, which lists the most commonly used prefixes and suffixes in printed school English.[21]

The Most Frequent Affixes in Printed School English

Rank	Prefix	% of All Prefixed Words	Suffix	% of All Suffixed Words
1.	*un-*	26	*-s, -es*	31
2.	*re-*	14	*-ed*	20
3.	*in-, im-, il-, ir- (not)*	11	*-ing*	14
4.	*dis-*	7	*-ly*	7
5.	*en-, em-*	4	*-er, -or (agent)*	4
6.	*non-*	4	*-ion, -tion, -ation, -ition*	4
7.	*in-, im- (in)*	3	*-able, -ible*	2
8.	*over-*	3	*-al, -ial*	1
9.	*mis-*	3	*-y*	1
10.	*sub-*	3	*-ness*	1
11.	*pre-*	3	*-ity, -ty*	1
12.	*inter-*	3	*-ment*	1
13.	*fore-*	3	*-ic*	1
14.	*de-*	2	*-ous, -eous, -ious*	1
15.	*trans-*	2	*-en*	1
16.	*super-*	1	*-er (comparative)*	1
17.	*semi-*	1	*-ive, -ative, -tive*	1
18.	*anti-*	1	*-ful*	1
19.	*mid-*	1	*-less*	1
20.	*under- (too little)*	1	*-est*	1
	All Others	3	All Others	1

Suffixes have less stable meanings, so merely learning their abstract definitions can be confusing. But learning to recognize common suffixes such as *-tion, -less, -ed,* and *-ing* will help students understand a word's function. For example, remembering that *-tion* indicates the word is a noun and that *-ed* usually forms the past tense of verbs can make it easier for readers to figure out words with these suffixes. Providing plenty of examples of suffixed words is probably more useful than memorizing the definitions of suffixes.[22]

Once students have grasped the concepts of roots, prefixes, and suffixes, you can more easily teach them specific word parts. Only 20 prefixes make up 97 percent of the prefixed words in printed school English. Sixty-five percent of suffixed words end in *-s, -es, -ed,* or *-ing*. Teaching your students to use just a few of these affixes can dramatically improve their vocabulary development. One study found that third graders who were taught the first nine prefixes in the chart and how to break down words into roots and suffixes outperformed a control group tested in measures of word meaning. [23]

Many lists of Greek and Latin roots are available online and in various publications. While not all of them are as useful as prefixes and suffixes—in part because meanings have changed over the centuries—they can still provide valuable knowledge to unlocking meaning, particularly in scientific words and in words involving numbers. Using word webs like the one shown here can reinforce the relation among words incorporating these roots.

Word Part Web

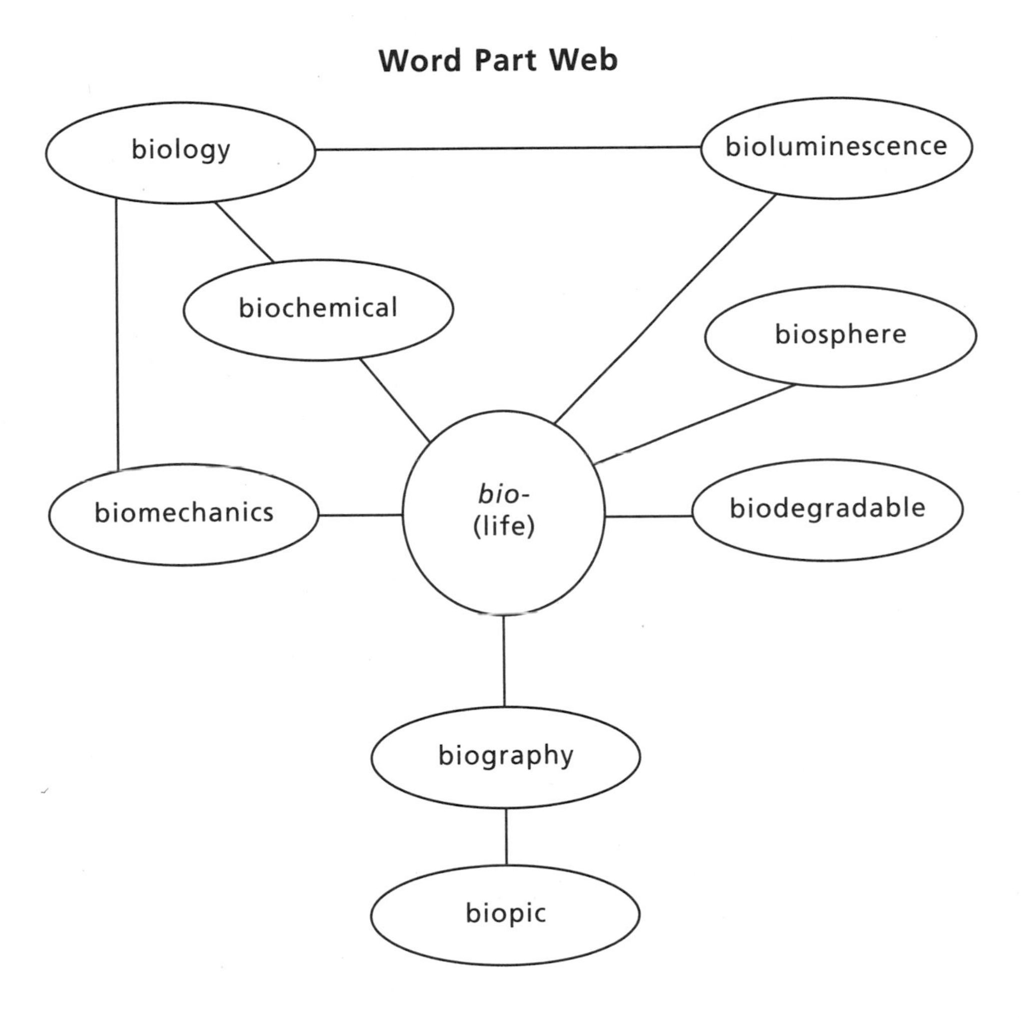

The strategy of using word parts is probably most effective when combined with other ways of acquiring words, such as using context clues. Knowing how to break down words into parts will make them easier to tackle; learning prefixes, suffixes, and some roots will give students more tools for vocabulary growth.

Use Graphic Organizers

Encouraging wide reading, using context, and employing word parts are excellent long-term strategies for vocabulary development. This section provides some additional activities that can deepen your students' word knowledge and expand your direct instruction of vocabulary.

Note: The four graphic organizers shown in the following pages are available to download in the "Educators" section of the free www.WordlyWise3000.com website.

Concept of Definition Maps

Concept of definition maps such as the one below are graphic organizers that show the elements of a typical dictionary definition, including:

- The category to which the word belongs, labeled, "What is this?"
- Characteristics of the word, labeled, "What is it like?"
- Examples and non-examples of the word.[24]

Students fill in the maps by referring to context, using their prior knowledge, and consulting dictionaries. The following map elucidates the meaning of *portion,* which appears in Book 4, Lesson 8:

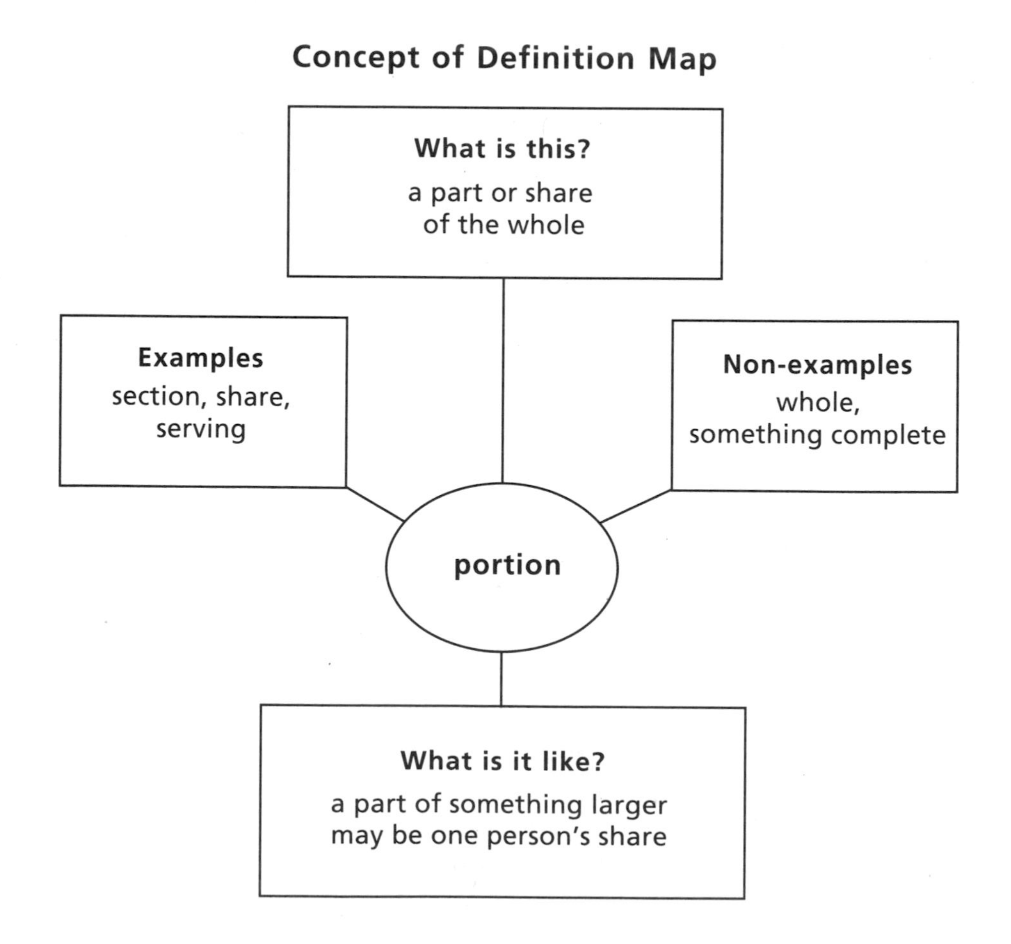

After having the class complete the map, you may want to model how to write a definition using the information in the map. For example, you could say, "A portion is a part or share of a whole. It might be a section of something or one person's serving of food." You can also have students write their own definitions and then confirm them by looking up the word in the dictionary. They may revise their definitions after looking them up.

Semantic Maps

Semantic maps can be used to develop students' understanding of a particular concept or group of thematically related words.[25] For example, in teaching an essay about the Great Wall of China, you might target the following vocabulary words: *barrier, threat, external, frontier,* and *breadth*. Then, begin instruction by having students brainstorm words related to the concept. As they brainstorm, list their words on the board, making sure to include the words you have targeted for them to learn.

Discussion is key to semantic mapping. During the brainstorming session, have students discuss and define all of the words. Help students refine their understanding of the words by asking them to group related words together to create a semantic map such as this one:

Semantic Map

Great Wall of China

- **barrier** blockade protection
- **threat** from outsiders **external** attacks
- border edge of territory **frontier**
- (blank)
- huge very long huge **breadth**
- (blank)

You might boldface the target words and leave sections blank so that students can fill in other categories after reading the selection. Semantic mapping is a great technique to use in content-area teaching, in which vocabulary words are likely to be thematically related. The technique works best as a group activity, since discussion provides information for students with smaller vocabularies and provides advanced learners with another exposure to the vocabulary.

Semantic Feature Analysis

Another good technique to use in teaching related words is semantic feature analysis, which makes use of a grid like the following.[26] The left-hand column contains the names of members of the category.

Semantic Feature Analysis

	has fur	has feathers	can fly	can be a pet	runs on four legs
dog	+	-	-	+	+
cat	+	-	-	+	+
hamster	+	-	-	+	+
buffalo	?	-	-	-	+
tiger	+	-	-	-	+
sparrow	-	+	+	-	-
horse	?	-	-	?	+

For a unit on living creâtures, you might write words such as *dog, cat, hamster, buffalo, tiger, sparrow,* and *horse.* The top row of the grid names features of the category's members such as *has fur, has feathers, can fly, can be a pet,* and *runs on four legs.* Encourage students to add terms to either column or row titles during discussion.

After seeing the grid, discuss whether the items in the column are an example of the features across the top, marking + for positive examples, – for negative examples, and ? for words that *might* be examples. As with semantic maps, discussion is key to clarifying the meanings of words in this activity, and for changing the ?'s to +'s or –'s. It is also an excellent technique to use in content areas such as social studies and science.

Compare and Contrast: Venn Diagrams

A Venn diagram is another good graphic organizer to use, especially when teaching students to compare and contrast related concepts such as *trip* and *sojourn, virus* and *bacteria, nation* and *country,* and *poetry* and *prose.* Using a Venn diagram can help students discover the slight differences that make synonyms have only *nearly* the same meanings, as well as degrees of difference in meaning that denote various connotations. The following diagram helps to clarify the similarities and differences between two related concepts:

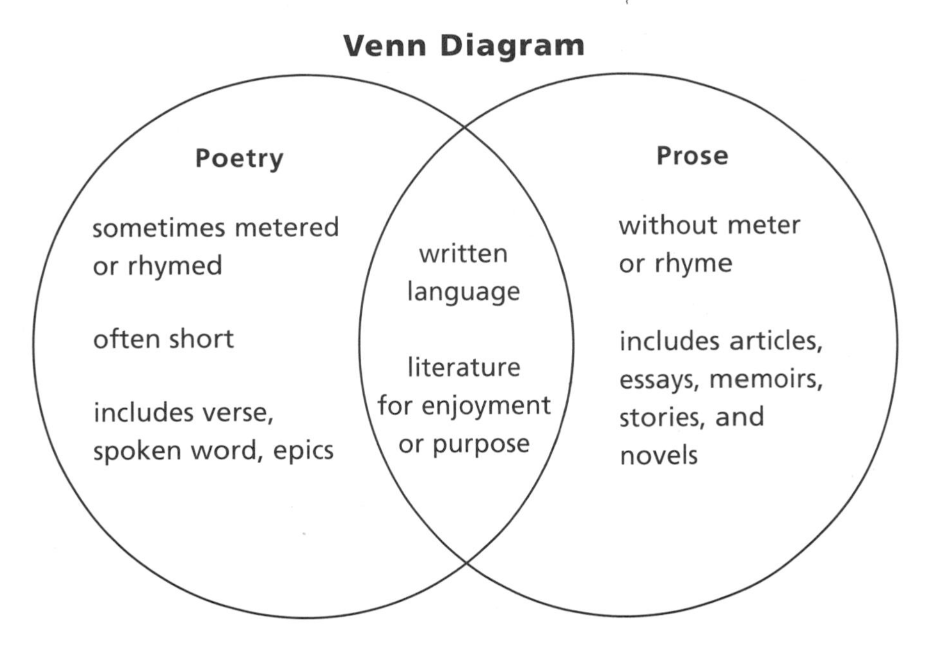

Using graphic organizers will provide your students with more exposures to words they are acquiring and will help them solidify the knowledge they've gained.

Extend Instruction through Reading Aloud and Discussion

Reading literature to students exposes them to rich language, sometimes referred to as "book language" or "academic language," that they usually do not hear in everyday speech. Reading nonfiction materials aloud to students exposes them to content-area, or domain, words, which they need to be successful in school. These are Beck et al.'s Tier Two and Tier Three words discussed earlier in this Guide.

Reading aloud is a common practice in the lower grades; in fact, reading aloud, in conjunction with using picture cues, forms the basis for *Wordly Wise 3000* K–1. Although research states that reading volume, rather than oral language, is the prime contributor to differences in students' vocabularies past the fourth grade,[27] additional research indicates that sixth graders learned about as many words from a single listening as they would from a single reading.[28] So, reading aloud can be a beneficial strategy to use even with older students, especially struggling readers, English language learners, and those with smaller vocabularies.

Discussion can greatly enhance any vocabulary instruction. Students with small vocabularies benefit from the knowledge contributed by their classmates, and misunderstandings of words can be cleared up as they surface. In addition, as students wait to be called on, they often practice responses silently. As a result, discussion reinforces vocabulary development.[29] Discussions can be made more fun by having students act out or pantomime words or debate word meanings.

Since vocabulary growth is a long process, drawing on a variety of approaches will help prevent boredom. As you use the strategies and techniques just described, you will be able to determine which ones will best help your students.

Chapter 3

Teaching a *Wordly Wise 3000*® Lesson

This chapter provides a guide to teaching a *Wordly Wise 3000* lesson. These instructions will help you introduce the basic concepts and approaches used in the lessons and will also help you extend the lessons, using the strategies and techniques discussed in Chapter 2. The lesson structure shown here and the approaches used are applicable to Levels 4 through 8 of *Wordly Wise 3000*.

Each Student Book in the series contains 20 lessons (15 in Books 2 and 3). Each lesson teaches 15 words (10 in Books 2 and 3) and may also teach various forms of a word, such as *patriot/patriotism/patriotic*.

Word List

Each lesson opens with a Word List that gives each word's definition(s), pronunciation, and sentences showing the words in context. Sentences are designed to provide meaningful context whenever possible. Since words are generally acquired in word families or related by roots, related word forms are presented in boldfaced type where appropriate.

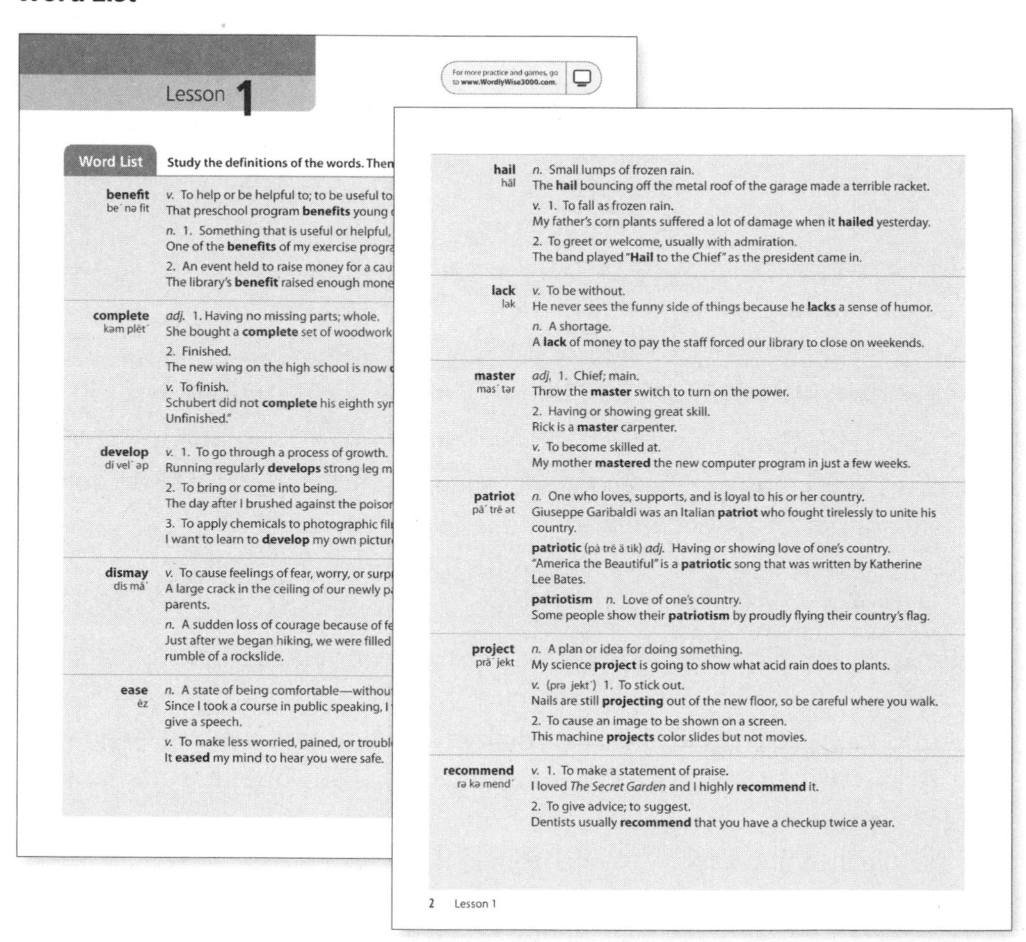

Lesson 1

For more practice and games, go to www.WordlyWise3000.com.

Word List Study the definitions of the words. Then

benefit be´ nə fit
v. To help or be helpful to; to be useful to
That preschool program **benefits** young
n. 1. Something that is useful or helpful,
One of the **benefits** of my exercise progra
2. An event held to raise money for a cau
The library's **benefit** raised enough mone

complete kəm plēt´
adj. 1. Having no missing parts; whole.
She bought a **complete** set of woodwork
2. Finished.
The new wing on the high school is now
v. To finish.
Schubert did not **complete** his eighth sy
Unfinished."

develop di vel´ əp
v. 1. To go through a process of growth.
Running regularly **develops** strong leg m
2. To bring or come into being.
The day after I brushed against the poiso
3. To apply chemicals to photographic fil
I want to learn to **develop** my own pictur

dismay dis mā´
v. To cause feelings of fear, worry, or surp
A large crack in the ceiling of our newly p
parents.
n. A sudden loss of courage because of f
Just after we began hiking, we were filled
rumble of a rockslide.

ease ēz
n. A state of being comfortable—withou
Since I took a course in public speaking, I
give a speech.
v. To make less worried, pained, or troubl
It **eased** my mind to hear you were safe.

hail hāl
n. Small lumps of frozen rain.
The **hail** bouncing off the metal roof of the garage made a terrible racket.
v. 1. To fall as frozen rain.
My father's corn plants suffered a lot of damage when it **hailed** yesterday.
2. To greet or welcome, usually with admiration.
The band played "**Hail** to the Chief" as the president came in.

lack lak
v. To be without.
He never sees the funny side of things because he **lacks** a sense of humor.
n. A shortage.
A **lack** of money to pay the staff forced our library to close on weekends.

master mas´ tər
adj. 1. Chief; main.
Throw the **master** switch to turn on the power.
2. Having or showing great skill.
Rick is a **master** carpenter.
v. To become skilled at.
My mother **mastered** the new computer program in just a few weeks.

patriot pā´ trē ət
n. One who loves, supports, and is loyal to his or her country.
Giuseppe Garibaldi was an Italian **patriot** who fought tirelessly to unite his country.
patriotic (pā trē ä tik) *adj.* Having or showing love of one's country.
"America the Beautiful" is a **patriotic** song that was written by Katherine Lee Bates.
patriotism *n.* Love of one's country.
Some people show their **patriotism** by proudly flying their country's flag.

project prä´ jekt
n. A plan or idea for doing something.
My science **project** is going to show what acid rain does to plants.
v. (prə jekt´) 1. To stick out.
Nails are still **projecting** out of the new floor, so be careful where you walk.
2. To cause an image to be shown on a screen.
This machine **projects** color slides but not movies.

recommend re kə mend´
v. 1. To make a statement of praise.
I loved *The Secret Garden* and I highly **recommend** it.
2. To give advice; to suggest.
Dentists usually **recommend** that you have a checkup twice a year.

2 Lesson 1

Begin by having students look at the Word List for the lesson. If this is the first time they have used *Wordly Wise 3000*, tell them that each lesson opens with a list of 15 words that they will discuss and learn, and that the Word List will be followed by several exercises. Point out that the Word List appears in a box on each subsequent two-page spread throughout the lesson, so that students don't need to continually flip back and forth to see their word choices.

Tell students that each Word List provides definitions as well as sample sentences. You may want to discuss the Word List as a class. Point out that each word's pronunciation is given beneath it and that each definition includes the word's part of speech. Explain that some words have more than one part of speech, as does the first word, *benefit*, which is both a verb and a noun. Also tell them that many words have more than one meaning. Note that sometimes several forms of a word are given in boldface type, such as *patriot, patriotic,* and *patriotism*.

Read aloud each definition and sentence for the first word, *benefit*. Point out that the sample sentences usually contain context clues to the meanings of the words. For example, for the noun form of *benefit,* the phrase "that I sleep better" provides an example of what a *benefit* is. Since this is the first lesson, you may want to go through all the words in a similar manner. In subsequent lessons, you can decide whether to continue this routine or to have students study the words on their own. To reinforce the meanings of some words such as *hail* or *remark,* you may illustrate them on the board or pantomime them.

You can extend the introduction of some words by using a concept of definition map. For *utter,* draw a blank map on the board and fill it in as shown below. Have students read the definition of *utter,* and then as a class, have them answer the questions in each box. Suggest that students consult a dictionary to supplement their knowledge. Write their answers in the boxes. Then, model how to write a complete definition of the word using the map. For example, you could say, "To utter is to speak or make sounds with the voice. When you utter, you express sounds that other people can hear." This map reinforces word meanings and can be used to provide students with extra practice at any point in a lesson.

Concept of Definition Map

What is this?
to make noises with the voice

Examples
to speak,
to talk

Non-examples
to mumble,
to be silent

utter

What is it like?
to make sounds,
to express in any way

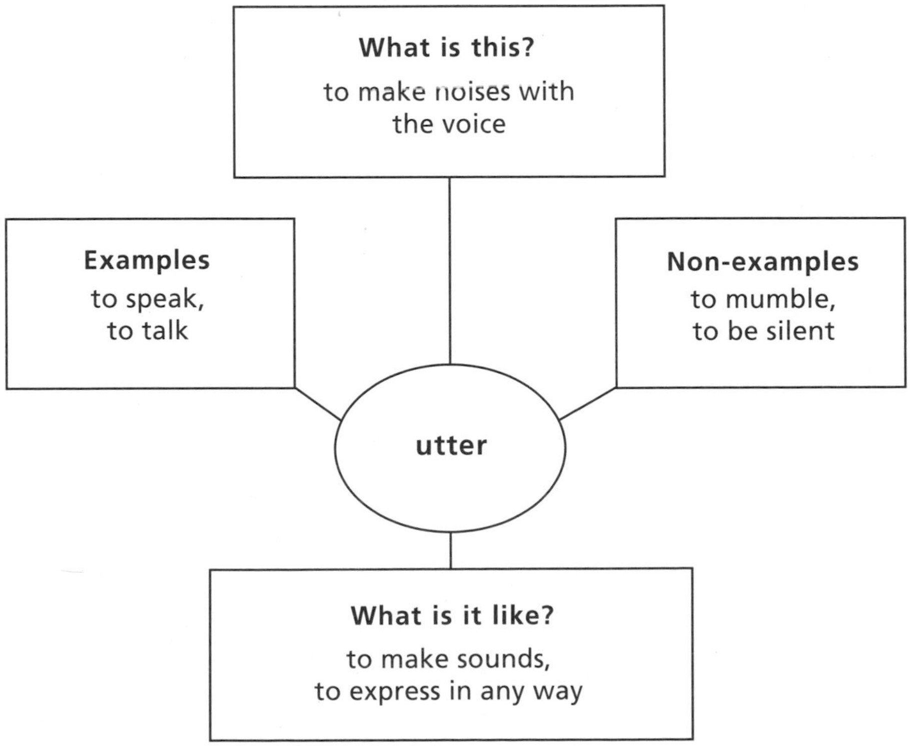

The Exercises

The introduction of the vocabulary words is followed by five exercises per lesson to reinforce the meanings of those words. These give students practice in applying the definitional or contextual information they have just seen in the Word List, helping them strengthen their understanding of each word's meaning.

The *Wordly Wise 3000* lessons work sequentially, with each exercise requiring more precise knowledge of the vocabulary words than the previous exercise. This systematic approach to vocabulary instruction enables students to actively participate in the process of their own word learning by thinking about the various meanings of each word and applying what they know.

Exercise A Finding Meanings

In the first exercise, Finding Meanings, students draw on their knowledge of the words' definitions to form sentences. The repeated use of words through this exercise and the ones that follow helps students build a full and flexible understanding of the vocabulary words.

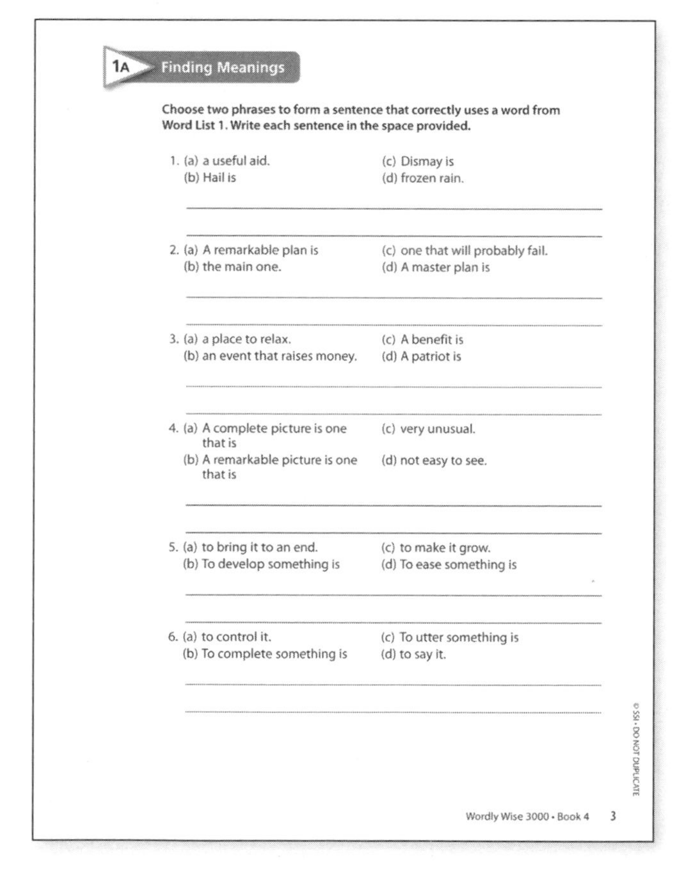

1A Finding Meanings

Choose two phrases to form a sentence that correctly uses a word from Word List 1. Write each sentence in the space provided.

1. (a) a useful aid. (c) Dismay is
   (b) Hail is (d) frozen rain.

2. (a) A remarkable plan is (c) one that will probably fail.
   (b) the main one. (d) A master plan is

3. (a) a place to relax. (c) A benefit is
   (b) an event that raises money. (d) A patriot is

4. (a) A complete picture is one that is (c) very unusual.
   (b) A remarkable picture is one that is (d) not easy to see.

5. (a) to bring it to an end. (c) to make it grow.
   (b) To develop something is (d) To ease something is

6. (a) to control it. (c) To utter something is
   (b) To complete something is (d) to say it.

Tell students to pick two of the four phrases to form a sentence that makes sense. Remind them to use the definitions from the Word List to answer these items.

For item 1, tell students to begin by looking at the four options: a, b, c, and d. Ask them, "Which two options can begin a sentence?" Say that since b and c begin with capital letters and can start the sentence, they should try combining these two options with the remaining ones to see if they make sense.

Model trying out different combinations by writing the following sentences on the board:

- Hail is a useful aid.
- Hail is frozen rain.
- Dismay is a useful aid.
- Dismay is frozen rain.

Have students discuss the sentences and choose the correct answer ("Hail is frozen rain."). As a class, have students complete the rest of the items, and answer any questions students have about the exercise.

Exercise B Just the Right Word

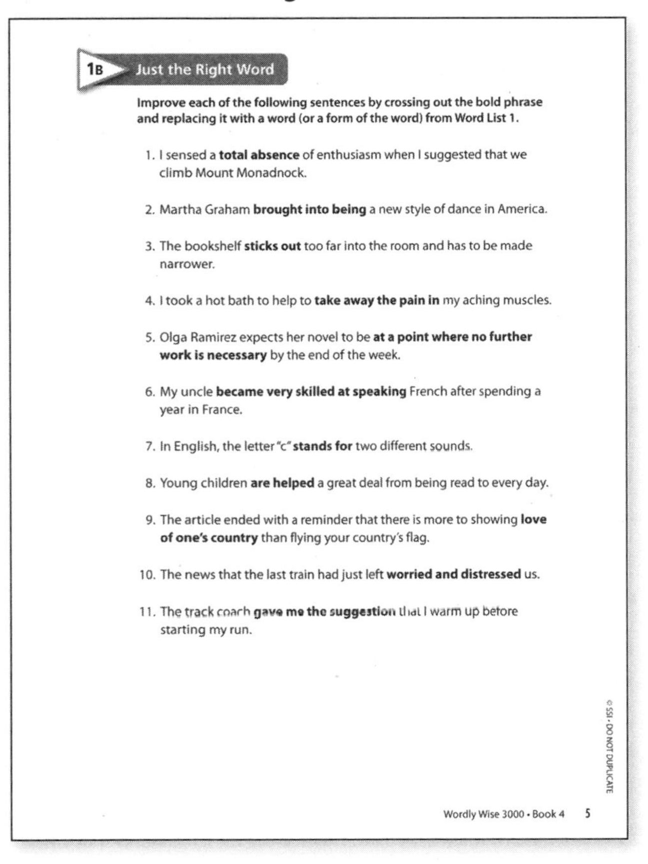

1B Just the Right Word

Improve each of the following sentences by crossing out the bold phrase and replacing it with a word (or a form of the word) from Word List 1.

1. I sensed a **total absence** of enthusiasm when I suggested that we climb Mount Monadnock.
2. Martha Graham **brought into being** a new style of dance in America.
3. The bookshelf **sticks out** too far into the room and has to be made narrower.
4. I took a hot bath to help to **take away the pain in** my aching muscles.
5. Olga Ramirez expects her novel to be **at a point where no further work is necessary** by the end of the week.
6. My uncle **became very skilled at speaking** French after spending a year in France.
7. In English, the letter "c" **stands for** two different sounds.
8. Young children **are helped** a great deal from being read to every day.
9. The article ended with a reminder that there is more to showing **love of one's country** than flying your country's flag.
10. The news that the last train had just left **worried and distressed** us.
11. The track coach **gave me the suggestion** that I warm up before starting my run.

© SSI • DO NOT DUPLICATE

Wordly Wise 3000 • Book 4 5

In the second exercise, Just the Right Word, students replace definitions of the words as they appear in sentences with the correct vocabulary words.

Read the instructions aloud and write the first sentence on the board. Read it and ask students what word from the list has the same meaning as "total absence." Cross out this phrase and write *lack* above it. You may want to repeat these steps with several items and then have students complete the rest of the exercise on their own.

You can extend this activity by having students come up with antonyms for some of the words after they have completed the exercise. Not all words have antonyms, of course, but thinking about antonyms requires students to consider crucial aspects of a word. In this exercise, you might have students identify the antonyms for *lack, complete,* and *dismayed.* Possible antonyms include *abundance, unfinished, happy.*

Exercise C Applying Meanings

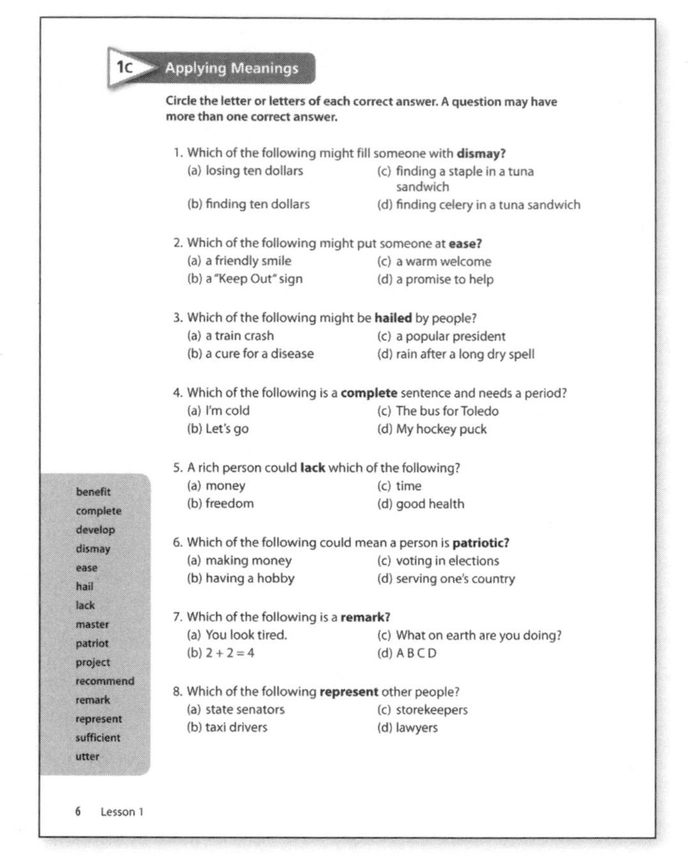

1C Applying Meanings

Circle the letter or letters of each correct answer. A question may have more than one correct answer.

1. Which of the following might fill someone with **dismay?**
   (a) losing ten dollars
   (b) finding ten dollars
   (c) finding a staple in a tuna sandwich
   (d) finding celery in a tuna sandwich
2. Which of the following might put someone at **ease?**
   (a) a friendly smile
   (b) a "Keep Out" sign
   (c) a warm welcome
   (d) a promise to help
3. Which of the following might be **hailed** by people?
   (a) a train crash
   (b) a cure for a disease
   (c) a popular president
   (d) rain after a long dry spell
4. Which of the following is a **complete** sentence and needs a period?
   (a) I'm cold
   (b) Let's go
   (c) The bus for Toledo
   (d) My hockey puck
5. A rich person could **lack** which of the following?
   (a) money
   (b) freedom
   (c) time
   (d) good health
6. Which of the following could mean a person is **patriotic?**
   (a) making money
   (b) having a hobby
   (c) voting in elections
   (d) serving one's country
7. Which of the following is a **remark?**
   (a) You look tired.
   (b) 2 + 2 = 4
   (c) What on earth are you doing?
   (d) A B C D
8. Which of the following **represent** other people?
   (a) state senators
   (b) taxi drivers
   (c) storekeepers
   (d) lawyers

benefit
complete
develop
dismay
ease
hail
lack
master
patriot
project
recommend
remark
represent
sufficient
utter

6 Lesson 1

In Applying Meanings, the third exercise, students answer questions that use the vocabulary words in a specific context. To select the correct answer, students need to use their full knowledge of each word's meaning.

Read aloud the instructions, and remind students that they can circle more than one answer—that is, more than one answer may be correct. Then have a volunteer read the first question and the possible answers. Have the class discuss whether or not and why each answer might be correct. Although a and c are the most probable answers to item 1, some students might be dismayed at finding *celery* in a tuna sandwich! Discussion will help students clarify the shades of meanings of the vocabulary words and will make this exercise more lively. To get the most out of the discussion, it's a good idea to call on many different students, so that the majority of the class will be silently preparing answers. You may wish to extend discussion throughout the exercise or have students complete the exercise on their own.

Exercise D Word Study

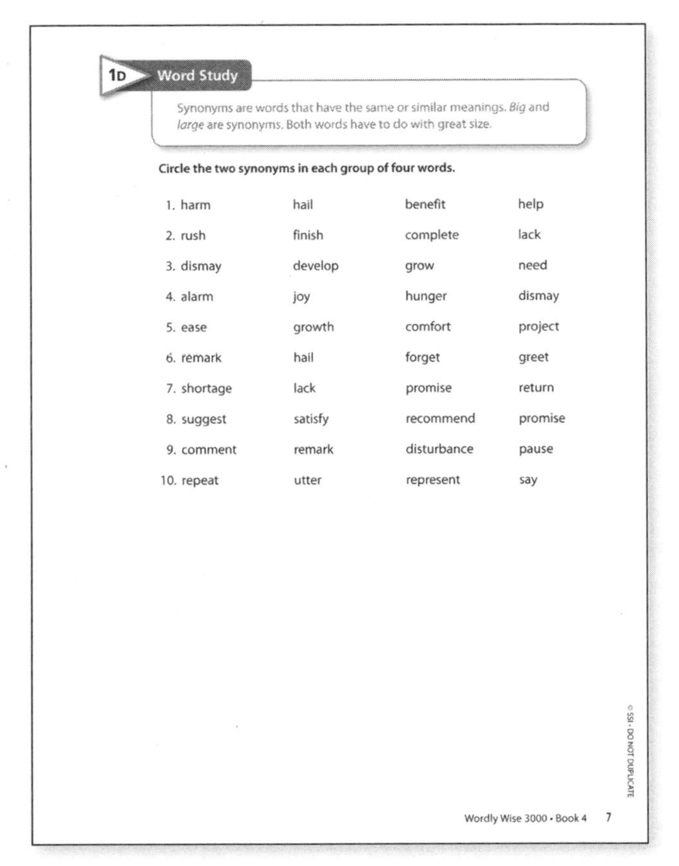

1D Word Study

Synonyms are words that have the same or similar meanings. *Big* and *large* are synonyms. Both words have to do with great size.

Circle the two synonyms in each group of four words.

1. harm	hail	benefit	help
2. rush	finish	complete	lack
3. dismay	develop	grow	need
4. alarm	joy	hunger	dismay
5. ease	growth	comfort	project
6. remark	hail	forget	greet
7. shortage	lack	promise	return
8. suggest	satisfy	recommend	promise
9. comment	remark	disturbance	pause
10. repeat	utter	represent	say

The fourth exercise provides more sophisticated word study. In the Word Study activity, students may identify synonyms and antonyms, explore how prefixes and suffixes change word meanings and parts of speech, learn about Latin and Greek roots, or distinguish between homophones. Solving Analogies begins in Book 6.

The Book 4 Lesson 1 Word Study exercise is about synonyms. Read the instructions aloud. Discuss the examples *big* and *large.* Ask students if they know any other words with similar meanings, such as *huge* and *massive,* and discuss the gradations of meaning of the words. Then discuss the meaning of *synonym,* noting that synonyms don't always have exactly the same meanings.

Read aloud the first set of words. Ask the class which items are synonymous. Use discussion to clarify the meanings of the words and the correct answer, *benefit* and *help.* Remind students to circle those words. Repeat this step with several items and then have students complete the exercise on their own. You can follow a similar pattern with the other Word Study exercises in this book.

Familiarize yourself with the various types of Word Study exercises in the book you are using so you can go over them with students as they get to each type.

Exercise E Passage and Questions

In the Passage, students read an original passage that incorporates all of the vocabulary words from the lesson. The vocabulary words are integral to the understanding of the text and thus contribute to students' comprehension rather than distracting them from the content by focusing on vocabulary.

1E Passage

Read the passage. Then answer the questions that follow it.

Sequoya's Gift

Sequoya was a **remarkable** man in many ways. He was a skilled silversmith and painter. He also served as a soldier. But he is remembered today for inventing a written language.

Sequoya was a member of the Cherokee nation, the son of a Native American mother and a British father. A **patriotic** person, he was **dismayed** that white people were taking over more and more of the Cherokee lands.

There was no easy way for Cherokees to be in touch with each other because they **lacked** a written language. Words spoken in Cherokee were lost as soon as they were **uttered.** Sequoya believed that the Cherokee people would **benefit** greatly if they had a written language and could read and write. Newspapers could spread the word of what was happening to people. Books could record their history. He made up his mind that he would try to **develop** a written language for his people.

The **project,** which he began in 1809, took twelve years to **complete.** He and his daughter worked together. She carefully sounded out each syllable. Then Sequoya **represented** each one with a letter that he chose from the English, Greek, and Hebrew alphabets. Eighty-six letters were **sufficient** to cover all the sounds of the Cherokee language.

Sequoya used this new written language in a message he sent to the leaders of the Cherokee nation. The leaders were impressed with how simple the system was. They **recommended** that the new written language be taught to everyone who wanted to learn to read and write. People liked it because it could be learned quickly and with **ease.** Those who **mastered** it went on to teach others. The Cherokees set up schools to teach Sequoya's alphabet and began to publish books and newspapers in their new language. The first Native American newspaper, the *Cherokee Phoenix,* was published on February 21, 1828. It was followed by a flood of other newspapers and books.

In his later years, Sequoya travelled throughout North America studying other Native American languages. Everywhere he went he was **hailed** for his invention, which played
people. He died in 1843. Hi
trees, and its beautiful Sequ

benefit
complete
develop
dismay
ease
hail
lack
master
patriot
project
recommend
remark
represent
sufficient
utter

8 Lesson 1

► **Answer each of the following questions in the form of a sentence. If a question does not contain a vocabulary word from the lesson's word list, use one in your answer. Use each word only once.**

1. How can we tell that Sequoya was **patriotic?**
2. What is the meaning of **utter** as used in the passage?
3. Why weren't any books written in Cherokee before 1821?
4. How did Sequoya feel about what the white settlers were doing?
5. What is the meaning of **develop** as it is used in the passage?
6. How did Sequoya use the English, Greek, and Hebrew alphabets?
7. Why weren't 26 letters **sufficient** for the Cherokee alphabet?
8. How long did Sequoya's work take?
9. Did Sequoya work on his **project** alone or did he have help?

Wordly Wise 3000 • Book 4 9

After reading the passage, students answer questions about it. If a vocabulary word is not used in the question, students must use it in their response. In this way, each word is reviewed once again.

The ultimate goal of the *Wordly Wise 3000* series is to have students develop vocabulary so that they can read with greater fluency and comprehension. By this point in the lesson, students have become well acquainted with the meanings of the words, so that the reading in context is in effect "debugged" for them. Most of the Passages are nonfiction and mimic the type of reading students do in their content-area texts and in nonfiction books.

Depending on your students' needs, you may want to read the passage "Sequoya's Gift" aloud or have volunteers do so.

Although the questions are about the content of the passage, students need to understand the meanings of the vocabulary words in order to be able to answer them. They must use complete sentences to answer the questions, and more subtle knowledge of how a word adapts to its context is required to answer some of these questions. Sample answers are given in the Answer Key in this Teacher's Resource Book.

Read the instructions that follow the passage, and clarify any questions students have about the exercise. Work together with the class to answer the first three items. Remind students that sometimes, as in question 3, they must use a vocabulary word in the answer, since none is used in the question. Have students complete the remaining exercises on their own or in small groups.

An alternative exercise has been provided in this Teacher's Resource Book beginning on page 15. While it is titled "Lesson Review Exercise," this cloze exercise can be used as a less challenging follow-up to the Passage, as a lesson extension (see page xxxiii), or for review or assessment.

If you use this cloze exercise, make copies for the students beforehand. Read the directions with students, and walk them through the first item, discussing their answers.

Fun & Fascinating Facts

This boxed feature appears at the end of each lesson, providing explanations or short stories about word origins and word families.

10. Why was the new language popular with the people?

11. How can we tell that the Cherokee leaders liked the new system?

12. What is the meaning of **hailed** as it is used in the passage?

13. How did the Cherokees help each other learn the new language?

14. What was **remarkable** about Sequoya?

15. How does a written language **benefit** friends living far apart?

benefit
complete
develop
dismay
ease
hail
lack
master
patriot
project
recommend
remark
represent
sufficient
utter

FUN & FASCINATING FACTS

- The Latin bene means "good" and forms a root of the word **benefit.** A *benefit* is something that is good for a person. Other words formed from this root include *benevolent,* which means "having a wish to do good" and *beneficial,* which means "doing good."
- In addition to its meaning as a verb, **utter** is also an adjective and means "total" or "absolute." (When the cellar door slammed shut behind us, we were left in *utter* darkness.); (I felt like an *utter* fool when the bike I reported stolen was found just where I left it.)

10 Lesson 1

Telling stories about words conveys a sense of fun about language and encourages students to become interested in learning words in general. You may wish to explain that English words are often derived from Latin, Greek, and other languages, which can sometimes help students figure out word meanings. Volunteers may read the feature aloud.

For Lesson 1, you may wish to have students brainstorm other words derived from *bene,* such as *beneficiary.* You may also wish to have students use the adjective meaning of *utter,* explained here, in sentences.

Extending and Reviewing the Lesson

Have students do the puzzle in groups or individually, but make sure to discuss the answers as a group.

Review Puzzle

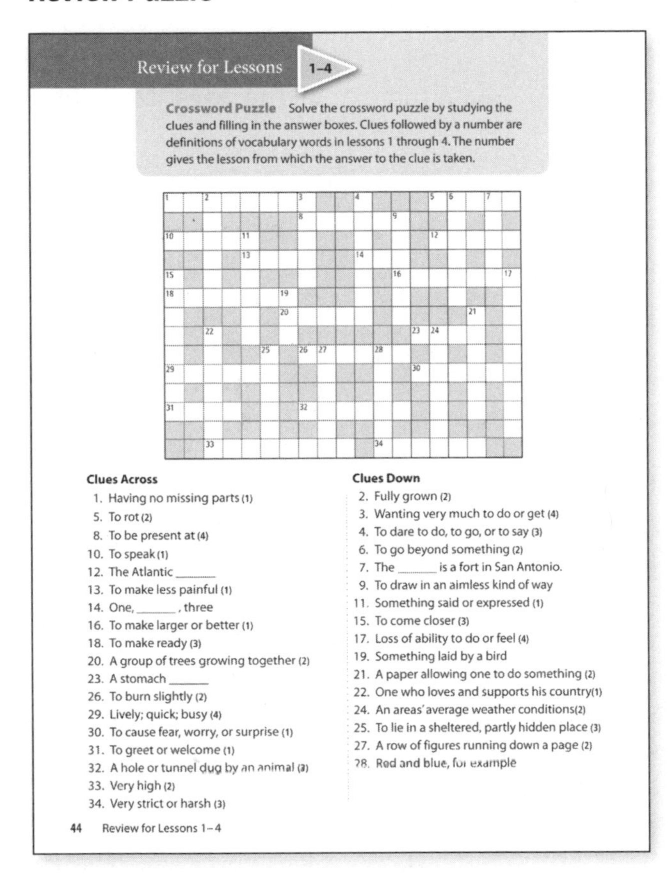

Review for Lessons 1–4

Crossword Puzzle Solve the crossword puzzle by studying the clues and filling in the answer boxes. Clues followed by a number are definitions of vocabulary words in lessons 1 through 4. The number gives the lesson from which the answer to the clue is taken.

Clues Across

1. Having no missing parts (1)
5. To rot (2)
8. To be present at (4)
10. To speak (1)
12. The Atlantic ______
13. To make less painful (1)
14. One, ______ , three
16. To make larger or better (1)
18. To make ready (3)
20. A group of trees growing together (2)
23. A stomach ______
26. To burn slightly (2)
29. Lively; quick; busy (4)
30. To cause fear, worry, or surprise (1)
31. To greet or welcome (1)
32. A hole or tunnel dug by an animal (3)
33. Very high (2)
34. Very strict or harsh (3)

Clues Down

2. Fully grown (2)
3. Wanting very much to do or get (4)
4. To dare to do, to go, or to say (3)
6. To go beyond something (2)
7. The ______ is a fort in San Antonio.
9. To draw in an aimless kind of way
11. Something said or expressed (1)
15. To come closer (3)
17. Loss of ability to do or feel (4)
19. Something laid by a bird
21. A paper allowing one to do something (2)
22. One who loves and supports his country(1)
24. An areas' average weather conditions(2)
25. To lie in a sheltered, partly hidden place (3)
27. A row of figures running down a page (2)
28. Red and blue, for example

44 Review for Lessons 1–4

Every fourth lesson is followed by a crossword puzzle or hidden message puzzle that incorporates a selection of words from the previous four lessons, giving students a playful way to revisit the words they now know as their own.

You may also use the cloze-format Lesson Review Exercises (see pages 15–55). An Answer Key is found on pages 57–59.

Testing and Assessment

Assess students' understanding by administering the corresponding Lesson Test. These reproducible tests, found in this Teacher's Resource Book beginning on page 61, test every word in all the forms and meanings taught. A cumulative Midterm (following Lesson 10) and a Final Test (following Lesson 20) each provide new passages using a selection of the words from the lessons. An Answer Key for the tests can be found on pages 167–170.

Another alternative is the *Wordly Wise 3000* Test Generator, available separately, which allows you to customize assessment by choosing only those words you wish to test, as well as providing the opportunity to test words from any group of lessons. The Test Generator also allows you to construct alternative forms of a test for security and/or for test–retest purposes, to differentiate instruction, and as a means of documenting learning gains.

Other Vocabulary Resources

Wordly Wise 3000® Online

For more than 15 years, educators have trusted *Wordly Wise 3000* to help them provide the best vocabulary instruction for their students. Now, with the release of *Wordly Wise 3000 Online,* educators have another option. Online technology offers a totally new experience that enhances vocabulary instruction in significant ways and makes it appropriate for whole new populations of students.

Wordly Wise 3000 Online is a new program that has all the advantages of the existing print program.

- Because *Wordly Wise 3000 Online* was developed with Universal Design for Learning (UDL) standards in mind, it is accessible to students at all levels of learning—struggling learners included.

- Because it offers robust audio scaffolding, immediate feedback, and remediation, *Wordly Wise 3000 Online* opens up an avenue of rich vocabulary instruction to students who are learning English.

- Because *Wordly Wise 3000 Online* is engaging and interactive, it appeals to today's tech-savvy student. Greater appeal means greater attention to content and therefore more effective learning.

- Because *Wordly Wise 3000 Online* provides both instruction and immediate feedback for all student exercises and activities in a seamless fashion, it can be a truly viable independent learning experience—anytime.

- Because *Wordly Wise 3000 Online*'s Learning Management System provides a robust reporting feature, educators need not sacrifice real-time monitoring of student progress for the independence gained by online learning.

Wordly Wise 3000 Online covers all the same material as the print edition, but provides scaffolding and enhancements that are unavailable in print, for both student and teacher, including more time on task for students and fewer demands on teachers.

Wordly Wise 3000® Online

Feature	Description	Benefit
Audio support	All words, activities, and feedbacks have audio. Students can click an icon to hear anything in the program read by a human voice with correct pronunciation and fluency.	For students struggling with pronunciation, meaning, and fluency, audio support is a very strong lifeline. Audio support also makes *Wordly Wise 3000 Online* ideal for helping English Language Learners and struggling readers match sound to text and pronounce words. English Language Learners in particular benefit from hearing fluent reading of all content.
Immediate feedback	As students answer any question (except in pre- and post-tests) in *Wordly Wise 3000 Online,* they receive corrective feedback, either confirming a correct answer or prompting them to provide the correct answer.	Feedback hints and features, such as making any incorrect answers students may choose inactive, always make the selection of correct answers attainable. Before moving on to subsequent questions, students must always supply the correct answer, leaving them with a feeling of success.
Interactivity and visual appeal	Designed for today's tech-savvy student, *Wordly Wise 3000 Online* provides an appealing, game-like interface without sacrificing the rigor and pedagogy of a robust vocabulary curriculum.	Strong motivation to use the program means greater attention to content and therefore more effective learning.
Assessment	A pre-test and post-test for every lesson allows you to monitor student progress. Performance reports on all tests and activities are available instantly through the reporting feature (see next page).	This allows the teacher to make decisions about student needs, including further intervention, before frustration sets in. Optional cumulative tests provide another opportunity for assessment.

Wordly Wise 3000® Online

Feature	Description	Benefit
Remediation	Whenever students miss a question on the post-test, they are automatically assigned "Master Meanings," a remediation activity for each word missed.	Students revisit words they failed to master while they are fresh in their minds and have another opportunity to learn the appropriate word meaning(s).
Assignment	Teachers assign students through an easy-to-use Learning Management System which sets up students for a full level's work and provides automatic reports. Adjustments in assignments can be made any time students need to be at a different level.	Students can work independently, with more time on task, while teachers are freed from time-consuming assigning and monitoring.
Reports	Class and individual student reports allow monitoring and documenting of student progress. Reports give information about activities and words that present problems for students.	For schools using RtI, this documentation is extremely useful. For all teachers, this time-saving feature allows them to stay on top of students' progress and to intervene, as needed, to address student learning problems.

Wordly Wise Science and Social Studies™

Wordly Wise Science and Social Studies, used in conjunction with *Wordly Wise 3000* or *Wordly Wise 3000 Online,* provides a total vocabulary solution for Grades 4–8.

While *Wordly Wise 3000*—in both formats—provides direct instruction in Tier Two vocabulary, *Wordly Wise Science and Social Studies* provides instruction in Tier Three words, that is, domain-specific words.

Wordly Wise Science and Social Studies is an all online program whose format resembles that of *Wordly Wise 3000 Online,* providing similar support and enhancements. It covers 500 content-area words (250 Science and 250 Social Studies) over five levels. Designed to be used in conjunction with the topics most frequently taught in Grades 4–8, the lessons can be arranged in any order to match up with the curriculum in any class.

Endnotes

[1] Southwest Educational Development Laboratory, 14; Stahl, 3.

[2] Biemiller, 24.

[3] Biemiller, 28.

[4] Stahl, 12.

[5] Stahl, 9; Texas Education Agency, 5–6.

[6] Stahl, 30.

[7] Beck et al., 8.

[8] Stahl and Nagy, 41.

[9] Stahl, 30; Texas Education Agency, 20.

[10] Texas Education Agency, 8.

[11] Hunt and Beglar, 1.

[12] Dale and O'Rourke.

[13] Stahl, 31–32; Texas Education Agency, 21–23.

[14] Texas Education Agency, 14.

[15] Texas Education Agency, 19.

[16] Stahl, 11, 28–29.

[17] Texas Education Agency, 20.

[18] Beck et al., 118–120.

[19] Biemiller, 28.

[20] Texas Education Agency, 40.

[21] Texas Education Agency, 36–38.

[22] Stahl and Nagy, 164.

[23] Stahl, 45.

[24] Schwartz and Raphael, 198–203.

[25] Heimlich and Pittelman.

[26] Stahl, 39–40; Texas Education Agency, 32–33.

[27] Southwest Educational Development Laboratory, 14.

[28] Stahl, 13.

[29] Stahl, 34.

Bibliography

Beck, I. A., McKeown, M. G., & Kucan, L. (2002). *Bringing words to life: Robust vocabulary instruction.* New York, NY: Guilford Press.

Biemiller, A. (2001). Teaching vocabulary: Early, direct, and sequential. *American Educator, 25*(1), 24-28, 47.

Common Core State Standards Initiative. (2010). *Common Core State Standards for English language arts & literacy in history/social studies, science, and technical subjects.* Washington, DC: National Governors Association Center for Best Practices and the Council of Chief State School Officers.

Dale, E., & O'Rourke, J. (1986). *Vocabulary building.* Columbus, OH: Zaner-Bloser.

Dalton, B., & Grisham, D. L. (2011). eVoc Strategies: 10 Ways to Use Technology to Build Vocabulary. *The Reading Teacher, 64*(5), 306-317.

Heimlich, J. E., & Pittelman, S. D. (1986). *Semantic mapping: Classroom applications.* Newark, DE: International Reading Association.

Hunt, A., & Beglar, D. (1998). Current research and practice in teaching vocabulary. *The Language Teacher, 22*(01). Retrieved from http://www.jalt-publications.org/old_tlt/articles/1998/01/hunt

Kelley, J. G., Lesaux, N. K., Kleffer, M. J., & Faller, S. E. (2010). Effective academic vocabulary instruction in the urban middle school. *The Reading Teacher, 64*(1), 5-14.

Marzano, R. J., & Pickering, D. K. (2005). *Building academic vocabulary: Teacher's manual.* Alexandria, VA: Association for School Curriculum Directors.

Schwartz, R. M., & Raphael, T. (1985). Concept of definition: A key to improving students' vocabulary. *The Reading Teacher, 39*(2), 198-205.

Southwest Educational Development Laboratory. (2000). T*he cognitive foundations of learning to read: A framework.* Austin, TX: Author. Retrieved from http://www.sedl.org/reading/framework/framework.pdf

Stahl, S. A. (1999). *Vocabulary development.* Cambridge, MA: Brookline Books.

Stahl, S. A., & Nagy, W. E. (2006). *Teaching word meanings.* Mahwah, NJ: Erlbaum.

Texas Education Agency. (2000). *Promoting vocabulary development: Components of effective vocabulary instruction.* Austin, TX: Author.

Student Book Answer Key

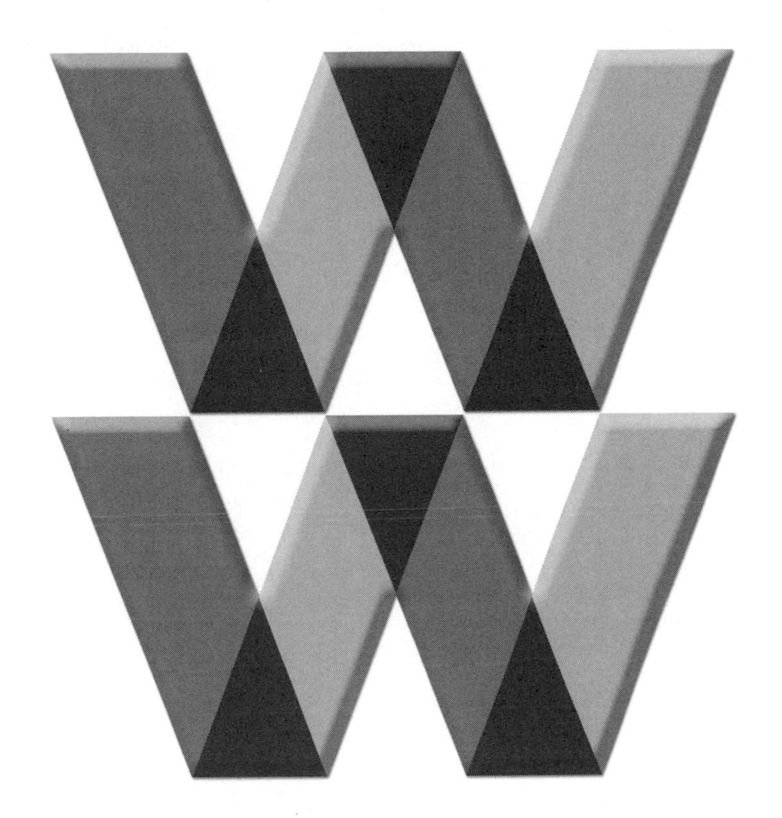

Lesson 1

1A Finding Meanings p. 3

1. c—a
2. b—a
3. b—c
4. d—c
5. d—c
6. a—d
7. d—a
8. b—d
9. a—d
10. c—a

1B Just the Right Word p. 5

1. obedient
2. retire
3. budge
4. compatible
5. alert
6. obstacles
7. distraction
8. assigned
9. pedestrians
10. patient

1C Applying Meanings p. 6

1. a, b, c
2. a
3. a, b, d
4. a, b, d
5. a, b, c, d
6. a, b, d
7. a, b, c
8. a, c

1D Word Study p. 7

1. budge—shift
2. retire—quit
3. barrier—obstacle
4. warning—alert
5. jostle—shove
6. alert—drowsy
7. slight—burly
8. unfamiliar—accustomed
9. obedient—defiant
10. retire—arise

1E Passage p. 8

(Possible answers; students' sentences may vary.)

1. The idea was that dogs could be trained to act as eyes for blind people.
2. It begins when the dog is **assigned** to its new owner.
3. Such a person might be more comfortable with a large, powerful dog.
4. They probably would not be very **compatible.**
5. People who are walking are usually on sidewalks.
6. Guide dogs are taught to disobey commands that would put their owners in danger.
7. This is done to **accustom** it to anything that might happen.
8. *Alert* means "watching out for signs of danger."
9. The dog will not **budge** until it is safe to do so.
10. They are trained to ignore **distractions.**
11. *Patient* means "willing to wait without complaining."
12. Garbage cans, mailboxes, and lampposts are some things that might be in the way.
13. They must make sure their owners don't get **jostled.**
14. *Retires* means "ends one's working life."
15. They are very close **companions.**

Lesson 2

2A Finding Meanings p. 14

1. a—b
2. d—b
3. c—d
4. a—c
5. b—d
6. c—b
7. c—b
8. c—a
9. d—a
10. b—d

2B Just the Right Word p. 16

1. beverages
2. extracts
3. exported
4. introduced
5. combination
6. cultivated
7. tropical
8. purchased
9. craved
10. cluster

2C Applying Meanings p. 17

1. a, c
2. c
3. a, c, d
4. b, d
5. a, c, d
6. a, b, d
7. b, c, d
8. b, d

2D Word Study p. 18

1. immature
2. unaccustomed
3. incomplete
4. incompatible
5. irresistible
6. disobedient
7. impatient
8. incapable
9. insufficient
10. disprove
11. dishonest
12. disengage

2E Passage p. 19

(Possible answers; students' sentences may vary.)

1. Eating some chocolate would satisfy a strong desire for it.
2. Cocoa is used to make chocolate candy and **beverages.**
3. *Cultivated* means "grown."
4. They cannot grow where it is cold and dry.
5. They are sent to countries all over the world.
6. They used them to **purchase** the things they needed.
7. Candy is made by **combining** cocoa powder with cocoa butter, sugar, and dried milk.
8. You would find a **cluster** of 20 to 40 cocoa beans.
9. The beans have a slight chocolate **aroma.**
10. *Consumed* means "drank."
11. After the beans are roasted, the shells become **brittle** and are easy to remove.
12. The cocoa butter is **extracted** from it.
13. Spanish explorers **introduced** chocolate to Europe in the 1500s.
14. *Bland* means "lacking a strong flavor."
15. They were **equivalent** in value for the Aztecs.

Lesson 3

3A Finding Meanings p. 25

1. b—a
2. c—a
3. b—c
4. b—c
5. c—d
6. d—b
7. d—a
8. d—a
9. c—d
10. c—b

3B Just the Right Word p. 27

1. obscured
2. puny
3. evident
4. ferocity
5. preyed
6. premature
7. survivors
8. option
9. duration
10. carnivores

3C Applying Meanings p. 28

1. c, d
2. a, b, c
3. a, b, c, d
4. c
5. a
6. a, c, d
7. a, c
8. a, c, d

3D Word Study p. 29

1. maturus: fully grown
2. vivere: to live
3. carnis: meat
4. ferox: fierce
5. pedester: on foot
6. cultus: plow
7. trahere: draw
8. prehendere: grasp
9. durare: to last
10. videre: to see

3E Passage p. 30

(Possible answers; students' sentences may vary.)

1. They found its remains **preserved** in rock in Utah.
2. It lasted over a hundred and fifty million years.
3. They became **extinct** about 65 million years ago.
4. They understand how it looked and how it attacked other creatures.
5. *Prey* means "an animal that is hunted for food."
6. *Tyrannosaurus rex* was **gigantic.**
7. *Survive* means "to stay alive."
8. There weren't really any possibilities for escape once *Utahraptor* attacked.
9. No. They were **puny** in comparison.
10. Scientists are still studying this subject.
11. It seems **evident** that it happened suddenly.
12. The dust from the meteorite would **obscure** the sun's rays.
13. The bones of a flying dinosaur have been discovered, leading some scientists to believe that it may be related to today's birds.
14. They were both **carnivores.**
15. It was a **ferocious** creature.

Lesson 4

4A Finding meanings p. 37

1. b—a
2. a—d
3. c—a
4. b—d
5. d—b
6. b—a
7. c—b
8. d—c
9. b—c
10. a—d

4B Just the Right Word p. 39

1. gales
2. navigating
3. destination
4. depart
5. voyage
6. horizon
7. approximate
8. course
9. severed
10. jubilant

4C Applying Meanings p. 40

1. a, b, c
2. a, c, d
3. a, d
4. a, b, c
5. a, b
6. a, c, d
7. a, b, c, d
8. a, b, d

4D Word Study p. 41

1.	deteriorate, improve	A
2.	jubilation, joy	S
3.	obvious, evident	S
4.	depart, arrive	A
5.	puny, burly	A
6.	correct, accurate	S
7.	comprehend, understand	S
8.	preserve, save	S
9.	separate, combine	A
10.	jubilation, despair	A

4E Passage p. 42

(Possible answers; students' sentences may vary.)

1. They were allowed to **depart** and practice their religion elsewhere.
2. *Sever* means "to break off."
3. The **voyage** lasted sixty-five days.
4. Their **destination** was Virginia.
5. *Accurate* means "able to give a correct reading or measurement."
6. There were about one hundred passengers on board.
7. The weather **deteriorated** after a couple of weeks at sea.
8. It would have been dangerous when strong **gales** rocked the Mayflower.
9. The trip seemed to take a long time. The bad weather made the trip very uncomfortable.
10. Cloudy skies would make it difficult for the crew to **navigate.**
11. They first saw it on the **horizon.**
12. *Revive* means "to become strong again."
13. They might have expressed their joy by cheering, laughing, or praying.
14. They might have felt a longing for their old friends, family, homes, and the towns they grew up in.
15. They had no choice but to begin building houses because it was the middle of winter.

Lesson 5

5A Finding Meanings p. 51

1. d—b
2. c—d
3. a—d
4. d—a
5. a—c
6. a—b
7. c—a
8. b—c
9. d—b
10. d—b

5B Just the Right Word p. 53

1. foolhardy
2. lure
3. summit
4. blizzard
5. route
6. conquest
7. crevice
8. challenge
9. optimism
10. makeshift

5C Applying Meanings p. 54

1. a, d
2. a, b, c, d
3. a, c
4. a, b, d
5. b, d
6. b, c, d
7. a
8. a, c

5D Word Study p. 55

1. assignment
2. distraction
3. craving
4. survivor
5. optimistic
6. horizontal
7. nostalgic
8. carnivorous
9. accuracy
10. jubilation
11. obedience
12. patience

5E Passage p. 56

(Possible answers; students' sentences may vary.)

1. It would be **foolhardy** to try such a thing.
2. *Challenge* means "something that takes skill or effort."
3. Any loud noise could start an **avalanche.**
4. Because the air is thin, climbers probably would say only what is necessary to save their breath for the climb.
5. The weather can change quickly for the worse, bringing **blizzards** or other dangerous storms.
6. Clear skies with little chance of snow would make a climber feel hopeful.
7. Into these rock openings, climbers drive spikes to hold their ropes for steep climbs.
8. *Route* means "the path that must be followed to get to a place."
9. It is best to try to set up a **makeshift** shelter.
10. They need ropes when they are climbing a **vertical** section of the mountain.
11. They would be **thwarted** in making the climb.
12. He said he wanted to climb it because it was there.
13. He had made several **previous** attempts.
14. They will have calculated the location carefully. They will probably see flags and other things left by climbers who were there before them.
15. They would feel happy that they had **conquered** the highest mountain in the world.

Lesson 6

6A Finding Meanings p. 62

1. d—a
2. d—c
3. d—b
4. b—c
5. d—a
6. c—a
7. a—c
8. b—a
9. b—c
10. a—d

6B Just the Right Word p. 64

1. monstrous
2. roused
3. agony
4. abolished
5. harbors
6. characters
7. grim
8. escalated
9. catapulted
10. inflicted

6C Applying Meanings p. 65

1. b, c, d
2. a, c, d
3. a, c, d
4. b, c
5. c
6. a, b, c
7. a, c
8. a, b, c

6D Word Study p. 66

1. defeat
2. cut
3. unclear
4. remove
5. correct
6. loyal
7. hatred
8. stern
9. short
10. weak

6E Passage p. 67

(Possible answers; students' sentences may vary.)

1. Many Americans supported slavery, but many others **loathed** it.
2. The quarrel **escalated** into a war.
3. President Lincoln **abolished** slavery in the United States.
4. Her novel *Uncle Tom's Cabin* **catapulted** her to world fame.
5. The plan to sell Eliza's child and the beating of Uncle Tom, which caused his death, were both terribly cruel acts.
6. The book was **translated** into many different languages.
7. Her interest in ending slavery was a concern for the basic well-being and fair treatment of an entire group of people.
8. She continued to **denounce** slavery in speeches, articles, and books.
9. *Character* means "a person in a story, movie, or play."
10. She probably hoped to **rouse** people into demanding an end to slavery.
11. *Harbor* means "to give shelter to and to take care of by hiding."
12. Eliza's pain came from her fear of what could happen; Tom's pain came from actual physical punishment.
13. He enjoyed **inflicting** pain on helpless people.
14. He **steadfastly** refused to tell where they could be found.
15. *Grim* means "unpleasant or disturbing."

Lesson 7

7A Finding Meanings p. 73

1. d—a
2. b—d
3. b—c
4. c—b
5. d—c
6. b—a
7. b—a
8. a—d
9. b—d
10. b—a

7B Just the Right Word p. 75

1. resemble
2. waddled
3. solitary
4. frigid
5. rigid
6. substantial
7. feeble
8. formal
9. remote
10. huddled

7C Applying Meanings p. 76

1. a, b, c, d
2. b, c, d
3. a, c, d
4. a, c
5. a, b, d
6. a, c, d
7. c
8. a, b, c

7D Word Study p. 77

1. gentle
2. joy
3. burly
4. fall
5. withdraw
6. flexible
7. boring
8. tropical
9. disloyal
10. love

7E Passage p. 78

(Possible answers; students' sentences may vary.)

1. People find them **fascinating** to look at.
2. *Deposit* means "to lay down."
3. Penguins do not fly in the air.
4. It looks like a very short man in **formal** dress.
5. Long ago, because they had no enemies to escape from, penguins had no reason to use their wings.
6. Summer temperatures are **frigid.**
7. They became excellent swimmers.
8. They spend a **substantial** part of their time in the water.
9. In the **remote** past, penguins were able to fly.
10. *Rigid* means "stiff and unbending."
11. The ice is two miles thick. The temperatures are always very low. No plants can grow to be used for nests.
12. By forming large groups, they are able to keep each other warm.
13. They **waddle** awkwardly on land but swim gracefully in water.
14. *Huddle* means "to crowd together."
15. A **solitary** penguin would quickly lose its body heat and die.

Lesson 8

8A Finding Meanings p. 84

1. c—b
2. b—d
3. d—b
4. a—b
5. d—c
6. b—c
7. a—d
8. d—a
9. b—d
10. d—c

8B Just the Right Word p. 86

1. frivolous
2. prospering
3. banquet
4. assembled
5. cargo
6. harvest
7. decrease
8. edible
9. desperate
10. hostility

8C Applying Meanings p. 87

1. c
2. c, d
3. a, c
4. a, b, c
5. a, b
6. a, c
7. a, b, c, d
8. a, b, c

8D Word Study p. 88

1. desperare: to give up hope
2. solus: alone
3. hostis: enemy
4. aequus: equal
5. proximus: nearest
6. frigus: cold
7. vivere: to live
8. portare: to carry
9. fascinare: to cast a spell on
10. fligere: to strike

8E Passage p. 89

(Possible answers; students' sentences may vary.)

1. Americans **celebrate** Thanksgiving every November.
2. They probably would think they were **frivolous.**
3. It carried a **cargo** of things that would be needed by the colonists.
4. They wrote the Mayflower Compact.
5. *Assembled* means "gathered together in a group."
6. They taught the pilgrims which berries and fruits were **edible** and how to grow different kinds of plants.
7. *Hewed* means "cut or shaped with blows of an ax or similar tool."
8. They made a **pledge** to be ruled by it.
9. The colonists probably served cider.
10. The liquid inside would run out.
11. The ripe crops they were able to pick probably included corn, beans, and squash.
12. The Native Americans were not **hostile** and a few could speak English.
13. The number of people had **decreased** to fewer than sixty.
14. They might have felt almost hopeless because nearly half of the people who came with them had died and their food was running out.
15. People would be better fed and clothed and would live in better housing.

Lesson 9

9A Finding Meanings p. 96

1. d—c
2. c—b
3. a—b
4. b—c
5. b—c
6. a—c
7. b—a
8. c—b
9. b—a
10. b—a

9B Just the Right Word p. 98

1. heroic
2. dense
3. mimics
4. absurd
5. soared
6. unwieldy
7. suspended
8. significant
9. experiment
10. lumber

9C Applying Meanings p. 99

1. a, b, d
2. a, c, d
3. b
4. a, c, d
5. a, c, d
6. a, b, c, d
7. a, b, c, d
8. c, d

9D Word Study p. 100

1. x
2. c
3. x
4. x
5. x
6. c
7. c
8. x
9. x
10. c
11. c
12. x
13. x
14. c
15. c

9E Passage p. 101

(Possible answers; students' sentences may vary.)

1. Hot air is less **dense** than cold air and therefore is lighter.
2. It is important because the first successful airplane flight was made there.
3. They built the first hot-air balloon that stayed in the air.
4. It **ascended** to a height of seventy feet.
5. They were too **unwieldy** to get off the ground.
6. *Soar* means "to fly high in the sky."
7. Members of the French royal family were among the **spectators.**
8. *Suspended* means "hanging while attached to something above."
9. Many of the early flights **terminated** in a crash.
10. The builders were trying to **mimic** the movement of a bird's wings.
11. They **experimented** with kites and gliders first.
12. *Lumber* means "to move in a clumsy or heavy way."
13. The planes became very **flimsy** and were more likely to crash.
14. A designer would probably think the idea **absurd.**
15. Today's airplanes are much safer than the very first ones.

Lesson 10

10A Finding Meanings p. 107

1. b—c
2. c—b
3. b—c
4. a—d
5. d—a
6. a—c
7. a—d
8. d—a
9. d—c
10. d—a

10B Just the Right Word p. 109

1. evade
2. available
3. reluctant
4. superior
5. pursuit
6. established
7. donations
8. occasion
9. prohibited
10. liberated

10C Applying Meanings p. 110

1. a, b, d
2. a, d
3. a, b
4. b, c, d
5. a, d
6. a, b, c, d
7. a, c
8. a, b, c, d

10D Word Study p. 111

1. ascend, rise S
2. end, terminate S
3. oppose, support A
4. lessen, decrease S
5. donate, receive A
6. flimsy, sturdy A
7. capture, liberate A
8. yearning, desire S
9. abolish, establish A
10. willing, reluctant A

10E Passage p. 112

(Possible answers; students' sentences may vary.)

1. It made it a crime to help runaway slaves.
2. *Superiors* means "people of higher rank."
3. She despised it and **yearned** to be free.
4. They were afraid of being caught and punished.
5. They **donated** money to help pay for her trips to the South.
6. *Evade* means "to keep away from; to avoid being caught."
7. She led her people out of **bondage** as Moses had done for the Jewish people in Egypt.
8. She might have reminded them that when they reached Canada, they would be free.
9. By providing safe places to stay, the stations on the Underground Railroad reduced the risk of capture.
10. They probably were **opposed** to slavery and wanted to help people escape from it.
11. It made these trips more dangerous because many people **pursued** her.
12. *Established* means "set up."
13. Education was not **available** to most slaves.
14. She worked as a nurse and **occasionally** acted as a spy.
15. She seems to have felt so strongly about the evil of slavery that she was willing to risk her life to free as many people as possible.

Lesson 11

11A Finding Meanings — p. 118

1. d—c
2. d—b
3. c—a
4. d—b
5. b—c
6. d—a
7. b—c
8. b—c
9. a—b
10. c—a

11B Just the Right Word — p. 120

1. maximum
2. proceed
3. exultant
4. solo
5. bracing
6. stall
7. contact
8. nonchalant
9. anxious
10. confidence

11C Applying Meanings — p. 121

1. c, d
2. a, b, c
3. a, b, c
4. b, d
5. a, b
6. a, b, c
7. b, c, d
8. a, b

11D Word Study — p. 122

1. con-
2. con-
3. con-
4. com-
5. com-
6. con-
7. con-
8. com-
9. con-
10. com-

11E Passage — p. 123

(Possible answers; students' sentences may vary.)

1. A **hangar** would be easily seen from the air.
2. The pilot can go no more than eighty-five miles per hour.
3. *Stall* means "to suddenly lose power."
4. Something might be overlooked, causing an accident.
5. The control tower **contacts** the pilot through the headphones.
6. *Confidence* means "a feeling of certainty or a lack of doubt."
7. The pilot tries to sound **nonchalant** while talking to the instructor.
8. The narrative says that the pilot **sauntered** over to the plane.
9. The pilot needs permission from the control tower.
10. About ten weeks of lessons are required before a **solo** flight.
11. The plane starts to **accelerate.**
12. It loses **altitude.**
13. *Brace* means "to make ready or to prepare for a shock."
14. The pilot might cheer or yell.
15. A person may feel **anxious** in the sense of worried or **anxious** in the sense of eager.

Lesson 12

12A Finding Meanings — p. 129

1. b—a
2. b—a
3. a—d
4. d—b
5. b—d
6. d—c
7. a—d
8. c—a
9. a—d
10. c—d

12B Just the Right Word — p. 131

1. restriction
2. penetrated
3. portrait
4. dictated
5. rebels
6. notable
7. convalesce
8. stimulated
9. dedicated
10. exasperating

12C Applying Meanings — p. 132

1. b, c
2. a, b, d
3. a, b, c
4. b
5. a, b
6. a, c, d
7. b, c
8. a, b, c

12D Word Study — p. 133

1. navigate, navigation
2. rebellion, rebellious
3. exasperate, exasperating
4. restrict, restriction
5. evade, evasive
6. fascinate, fascinating
7. celebrate, celebrated
8. prosper, prosperous
9. loathe, loathing
10. obedience, obedient

12E Passage — p. 134

(Possible answers; students' sentences may vary.)

1. The narrative says he was a **dictator.**
2. In 1910 they **overthrew** his government.
3. The narrative says Kahlo's parents gave their children a strict Catholic **upbringing.**
4. The new government tried to **stimulate** interest in the arts by supporting the work of artists.
5. They may have been annoyed because she supported the revolution and because she enjoyed doing things that shocked people.
6. *Overdue* means "coming later than expected or needed."
7. She liked to wear men's clothes.
8. This must have **restricted** her activities.
9. The spike **penetrated** her side.
10. While she recovered, she took up painting.
11. *Dedicated* means "set aside to honor her life and work."
12. The narrative says that she was **seldom** without pain for the rest of her life.
13. They had a **tempestuous** relationship with many separations.
14. She painted a number of **portraits** of her husband, her pets, and herself.
15. They were both **notable** Mexican painters.

Lesson 13

13A Finding Meanings — p. 141

1. d—b
2. a—d
3. c—a
4. d—a
5. b—d
6. b—a
7. d—c
8. d—b
9. b—c
10. c—a

13B Just the Right Word — p. 143

1. tapered (off)
2. rippled
3. gorge
4. accommodate
5. morsel
6. aggressive
7. carcass
8. flailed
9. sluggish
10. protruding

13C Applying Meanings — p. 144

1. a, c, d
2. a, c
3. a, c
4. a, b
5. b, c, d
6. b, c
7. a, b, c, d
8. a, d

13D Word Study — p. 145

1. visible, friendly
2. taper
3. protrude
4. none
5. sluggish, methodical
6. nonchalant
7. none
8. donate
9. evasive, burly
10. yearn

13E Passage — p. 146

(Possible answers; students' sentences may vary.)

1. The crocodile is a very **aggressive** animal.
2. A crocodile has a longer and narrower **snout.**
3. They both **slither** when moving on land.
4. The crocodile has a long, **tapering** tail.
5. Crocodiles hide the bodies of the animals they have killed so that they can return later to finish eating them.
6. They are likely to be **sluggish** when their surroundings are cool.
7. *Bask* means "to relax where it is pleasantly warm."
8. Only its eyes and nostrils can be seen.
9. It **flails** its tail to knock the animal off balance.
10. *Accommodate* means "to have room for."
11. The narrative says it **gorges** on the dead animal it has killed.
12. The crocodile can swim toward its prey without making a **ripple.**
13. They are above the surface so that the crocodile can see and breathe.
14. They eat **morsels** of meat that they pick from the teeth of crocodiles.
15. They hide themselves while they wait for thirsty animals to come to drink.

Lesson 14

14A Finding Meanings — p. 152

1. c—a
2. c—a
3. c—d
4. d—c
5. b—a
6. b—a
7. b—c
8. c—d
9. b—c
10. c—a

14B Just the Right Word — p. 154

1. wilderness
2. idle
3. taunted
4. decade
5. transform
6. delicate
7. provide
8. illuminates
9. tolerant
10. requirement

14C Applying Meanings — p.155

1. a, b
2. a, c, d
3. a, b, c
4. a, b, c, d
5. a, b, c, d
6. a, d
7. b, c
8. a, c

14D Word Study — p. 156

1. tri-
2. quad-
3. mon-
4. mono-
5. bi-
6. tri-
7. mono-
8. bi-
9. tri-
10. quad-
11. bi-
12. quad-

14E Passage — p. 157

(Possible answers; students' sentences may vary.)

1. It says that most of the state was still **wilderness** at that time.
2. It **provided** him with his first job.
3. Most people think of him as the inventor of the light bulb.
4. *Illuminate* means "to supply with light."
5. The other children used to **taunt** him for not joining in their games.
6. They probably climbed trees, wrestled, and played tag.
7. She took him out of school and taught him at home.
8. *Delicate* means "weak."
9. He had permission to sell newspapers and candy on board.
10. He used his free time to work on inventions.
11. *Idle* means "to spend one's time doing nothing."
12. He **transformed** it into a well-lit city by building the first electric power station there.
13. He must have had a **brilliant** mind to invent so many things.
14. One is **required** to obtain a patent.
15. He lived for over eight **decades.**

Lesson 15

15A Finding Meanings p. 163

1. b—a
2. c—b
3. a—d
4. a—b
5. d—c
6. c—b
7. a—d
8. a—d
9. d—a
10. a—c

15B Just the Right Word p. 165

1. fled
2. urban
3. disaster
4. lurch
5. fracture
6. petrified
7. major
8. intensity
9. prone
10. toppled

15C Applying Meanings p. 166

1. c, d
2. a, b, d
3. b, c, d
4. a, b, d
5. a, d
6. c
7. b, c, d
8. a, b, c, d

15D Word Study p. 167

1. tiny
2. minor
3. dim
4. sturdy
5. busy
6. reveal
7. often
8. shy
9. obedient
10. calm
11. mild
12. thick

15E Passage p. 168

(Possible answers; students' sentences may vary.)

1. They **investigate** the causes of earthquakes.
2. They measure the **intensity** of an earthquake.
3. There is still no way to **predict** when an earthquake will occur.
4. San Francisco lies on the San Andreas Fault.
5. *Topple* means "to fall over."
6. The ground often **lurches** during an earthquake, throwing people off balance.
7. *Minor* means "small or unimportant."
8. They might say they were **petrified** by what was happening.
9. An earthquake in such a place would be **disastrous.**
10. It would be a **major** earthquake.
11. Less damage will occur in a **sparsely** settled area.
12. **Fractures** in water pipes can cause flooding.
13. *Prone* means "likely to experience."
14. The loss of life was **immense.**
15. If you are in an old building that might collapse, you should leave it.

Lesson 16

16A Finding Meanings p. 174

1. b—d
2. b—d
3. a—d
4. d—c
5. b—c
6. b—d
7. d—b
8. b—c
9. d—a
10. a—c

16B Just the Right Word p. 176

1. next of kin
2. provoke
3. reigned
4. bungled
5. riot
6. guardian
7. proclaimed
8. dominate
9. assume
10. former

16C Applying Meanings p. 177

1. a, d
2. d
3. a, c
4. a, c, d
5. a, b, d
6. a, b, c
7. b, c
8. a, b, c, d

16D Word Study p. 178

1. propel
2. propose
3. produce
4. progress
5. project
6. proceed
7. proclaim
8. protrude
9. provoke
10. provide

16E Passage p. 179

(Possible answers; students' sentences may vary.)

1. It suggests that she finally accepted that Hawaii was part of the United States.
2. *Guardian* means "one who legally has the care of another person."
3. She expected to be **proclaimed** Hawaii's ruler.
4. Although her family was **kin** to the royal family, it was not in line to rule.
5. She was the widow of a **former** king and, therefore, would have had some experience with governing.
6. She represented her brother at Queen Victoria's Golden **Jubilee.**
7. Dole refused to obey President Cleveland.
8. They were to stop any **riots** in support of the queen.
9. Her supporters would be put to death if she did not give up her rule. If she did give it up, rule by the Hawaiian royal family would end completely.
10. *Assumed* means "took over the position of."
11. The rebellion that would have removed Dole from power was badly **bungled.**
12. They found weapons in her home; they said that messages between her and her followers had been **intercepted.**
13. She steadfastly denied **provoking** the rebellion.
14. *Pardoned* means "freed from legal punishment."
15. She **reigned** for less than three years.

Lesson 17

17A Finding Meanings p. 187

1. c—d
2. c—a
3. b—a
4. a—c
5. d—c
6. d—b
7. a—c
8. b—c
9. c—d
10. a—b

17B Just the Right Word p. 189

1. oasis
2. erosion
3. primitive
4. fertile
5. consists
6. expanding
7. teemed
8. afflicted
9. pasture
10. refugees

17C Applying Meanings p. 190

1. a, b, c
2. a, c, d
3. a, b, c, d
4. a, b, c, d
5. a, b, c
6. b, c
7. b, c, d
8. a, b, c, d

17D Word Study p. 191

1. idle
2. idol
3. taper
4. tapir
5. teem
6. team
7. reigns
8. reins
9. barren
10. baron
11. minor
12. miner
13. flea
14. flee

17E Passage p. 192

(Possible answers; students' sentences may vary.)

1. Deserts receive too little rainfall for anything to grow.
2. They become **refugees** in Southern countries.
3. Crops can be grown at **oases** because water is found there.
4. It has **expanded** south into the Sahel.
5. *Fertile* means "able to produce good crops."
6. Tropical rain forests are **teeming** with life.
7. The main cause is changed weather conditions.
8. *Primitive* means "simple or crude."
9. They starve because there is no **pasture** for them.
10. They **wither** and die.
11. The trees help to hold the soil in place.
12. With a change in weather patterns, they think it could **revert** to grassland.
13. The Sahel has recently been **afflicted** with the worst dry spells in nearly two centuries.
14. Apart from the central mountains, it **consists** mostly of sand.
15. They can prevent **famine.**

Lesson 18

18A Finding Meanings p. 198

1. b—c
2. a—b
3. a—c
4. b—c
5. a—d
6. c—b
7. d—a
8. b—c
9. b—a
10. c—d

18B Just the Right Word p. 200

1. retained
2. meager
3. obsolete
4. likeness
5. betrayed
6. sensation
7. negotiating
8. mischief
9. subsequent
10. vowed

18C Applying Meanings p. 201

1. a, b, d
2. a, b
3. b, d
4. a, b, c
5. a, b, c, d
6. b, c
7. c
8. b, d

18D Word Study p. 202

1. riot
2. rebellion
3. disturbance
4. uprising
5. uproar
6. tender
7. aching
8. sore
9. painful
10. agonizing

18E Passage p. 203

(Possible answers; students' sentences may vary.)

1. He had a **meager** income then.
2. He produced **animated** cartoons.
3. *Sensation* means "something that causes great interest or excitement."
4. He wanted to **negotiate** a better business deal for himself.
5. He had no money to **retain** a lawyer.
6. He **declined** all of them.
7. *Betrayed* means "to have been disloyal to."
8. The distributor had hired Disney's artists to draw Oswald cartoons for himself.
9. *Somber* means "sad or serious."
10. He **vowed** never to sell his movies in the future.
11. She saw the **likeness** between Mickey Mouse and her husband.
12. Most people probably preferred to have sound with their movies.
13. She **convinced** him that Mickey Mouse would be a better name.
14. All of Disney's **subsequent** films had sound.
15. They thought Mickey's adventures were **hilarious.**

Lesson 19

19A Finding Meanings p. 209

1. c—b
2. a—d
3. d—b
4. b—c
5. c—a
6. a—c
7. a—c
8. d—a
9. a—c
10. a—c

19B Just the Right Word p. 211

1. suffocation
2. eruption
3. population
4. fume
5. prelude
6. dormant
7. tremors
8. stupendous
9. excavation
10. expelled

19C Applying Meanings p. 212

1. c, d
2. a, c, d
3. a
4. b, c, d
5. a, c, d
6. a, b, c, d
7. a, b, c, d
8. a, b, d

19D Word Study p. 213

1. extract
2. exult
3. extinct
4. experiment
5. export
6. expand
7. expel
8. excavate
9. exasperate
10. exhale

19E Passage p. 214

(Possible answers; students' sentences may vary.)

1. They revealed the buildings, the objects used in daily life, and the bodies of the people who had died.
2. It had been **dormant** for so long that it did not seem dangerous.
3. *Prelude* means "something that comes before."
4. There were many public buildings and temples as well as **elegant** homes.
5. *Tremors* means "shaking movements."
6. The volcano **erupted** in a tremendous explosion.
7. The pressure inside the volcano had been building up for centuries.
8. **Molten** rock, or lava, as well as water and ash were thrown from the volcano.
9. *Expelled* means "thrown out with force."
10. The people had to work slowly and carefully to remove the dirt and volcanic ash without harming the objects underneath.
11. It was so hot that it **scalded** many people and animals.
12. It was filled with poisonous **fumes** and smoke.
13. He **perished** while trying to rescue his friends in Pompeii.
14. It had a **population** of about 20,000.
15. Many people were **suffocated,** while others were crushed or burned.

Lesson 20

20A Finding Meanings p. 220

1. d—b
2. a—d
3. b—c
4. c—b
5. b—c
6. b—a
7. b—c
8. b—d
9. c—a
10. b—c

20B Just the Right Word p. 222

1. burdened
2. resume
3. indignant
4. ridicule
5. jest
6. ample
7. comply
8. exertions
9. moral
10. encounter

20C Applying Meanings p. 223

1. b, c
2. a, b, d
3. a, b, c
4. b, c, d
5. b, c
6. a, b, c, d
7. c, d
8. b, d

20D Word Study p. 224

1. primitive, crude S
2. retain, keep S
3. animated, sluggish A
4. topple, overthrow S
5. pity, compassion S
6. mirth, laughter S
7. sparse, meager S
8. drab, elegant A
9. jest, joke S
10. careless, painstaking A
11. somber, jubilant A
12. die, perish S
13. decline, accept A
14. meeting, encounter S
15. barren, fertile A

20E Passage p. 225

(Possible answers; students' sentences may vary.)

1. They probably greeted it with **mirth.**
2. They would have arrived at the market with the father riding the donkey, and they probably would have been able to sell the animal.
3. He wanted to teach a **moral** to his listeners.
4. She has a very stupid father.
5. He was anxious to please everyone.
6. He **complied** with every one of them.
7. *Burden* means "a heavy weight that is carried."
8. He took her advice seriously because he didn't realize she had spoken in **jest.**
9. Being tied to a pole and carried must have troubled the donkey.
10. The donkey would be very **cumbersome.**
11. *Resumed* means "began again after a pause."
12. It says they were panting from their **exertions.**
13. *Ample* means "more than enough."
14. They were on the **outskirts** of the town.
15. They must have looked **ridiculous.**

Lessons 1–4

Hidden Message
pages 46–48

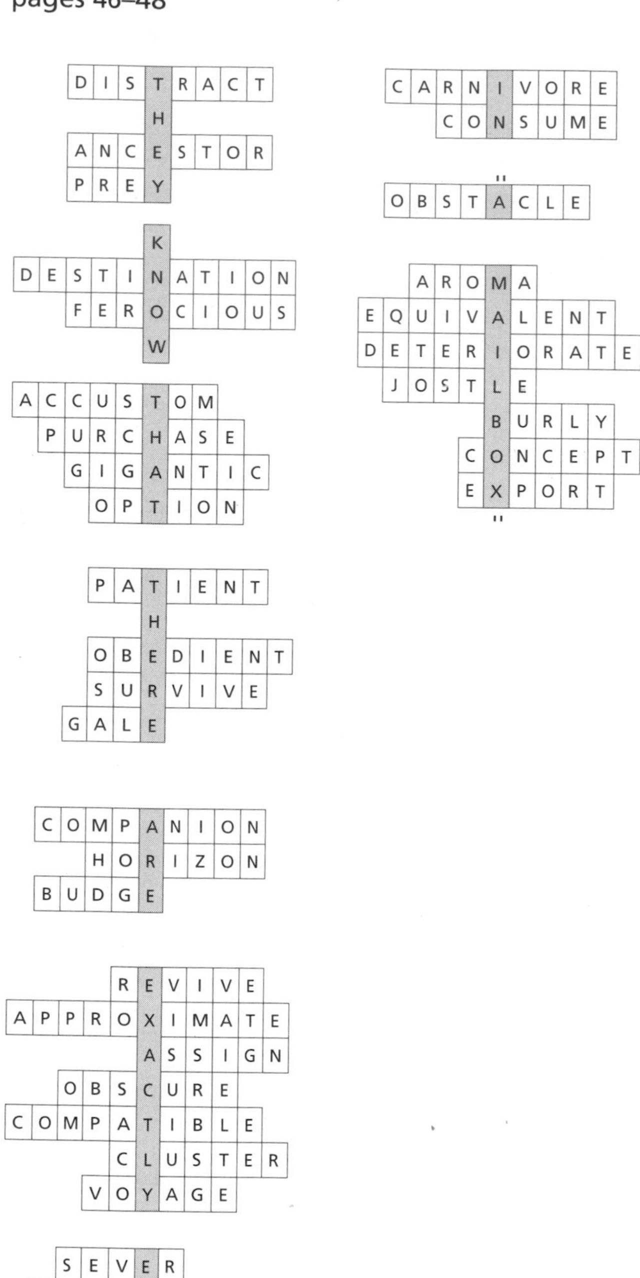

Lessons 5–8

Crossword Puzzle
page 93

1 S	U	2 M	M	3 I	T				4 G				5 H			
		A		N		6 D	E	C	R	E	A	S	E			
		K		F					I				7 W	E	8 A	K
9 F	E	E	B	L	E			10 O	M	A	11 H	A			G	
		S		I			12 M				O				O	
		H		C			O				S				N	
13 P		I		14 T	R	A	N	S	L	A	T	E		15 N	Y	16 C
R		F					S				I		17 W			R
18 O	P	T	19 I	M	I	S	T		20 L		21 L	O	A	T	H	E
S			N				22 R	O	U	T	E		D			V
23 P	L	E	D	G	E		O		R				D			I
E			I				U		24 E	D	I	B	L	E		C
R		25 H	A	R	V	E	S	T					E			E

Lessons 9–12

Crossword Puzzle
page 138

1 S	2 E	L	3 D	O	M							4 E	X	5 T	R	6 A
	V		E			7 P	U	R	8 S	U	E			E		S
9 S	A	U	N	T	E	R			O			10 M	I	M	I	C
	D		S			O			A					P		E
	E		E			C		11 B	R	12 A	C	E		E		N
13 R				14 O	V	E	R			D				S		D
E				V		E		15 D	E	D	I	16 C	A	T	E	
17 S	U	18 S	P	E	N	D		I				O				
T		A		R				C		19 B	O	N	D	A	20 G	E
R		T		21 D	O	N	A	T	E			T			L	
I		U		U				A			22 H	A	N	G	A	R
23 C	A	R	P	E	T			T				C			D	
T		N				24 S	P	E	C	T	A	T	O	R		

Lessons 13–16

Crossword Puzzle

page 184

1 T	O	2 P	P	L	3 E		4 A		5 V	6 I	S	I	B	L	7 E		8 I
		R			N		S			N					9 M	A	D
10 R	I	O	T		11 D	I	S	A	S	T	E	12 R			P		L
I		V					U			E		E		13 F	L	E	E
14 P	R	O	C	L	15 A	I	M			N		Q			O		
P		K			S		E			S		U			Y		16 P
L		E			S			17 P	18 R	E	D	I	C	T			R
E			19 M		O		20 M		E			R			21 D		O
	22 L		O		C		I		23 I	N	24 T	E	R	C	E	P	T
25 G	U	A	R	D	I	A	N		G		A				C		R
	R		S		A		26 O	W	N		P				A		U
	C		E		T		R			27 B	E	H	I	N	D		D
	28 H	E	L	M	E	T					R				29 E	V	E

Lessons 17–20

Hidden Message

pages 229–231

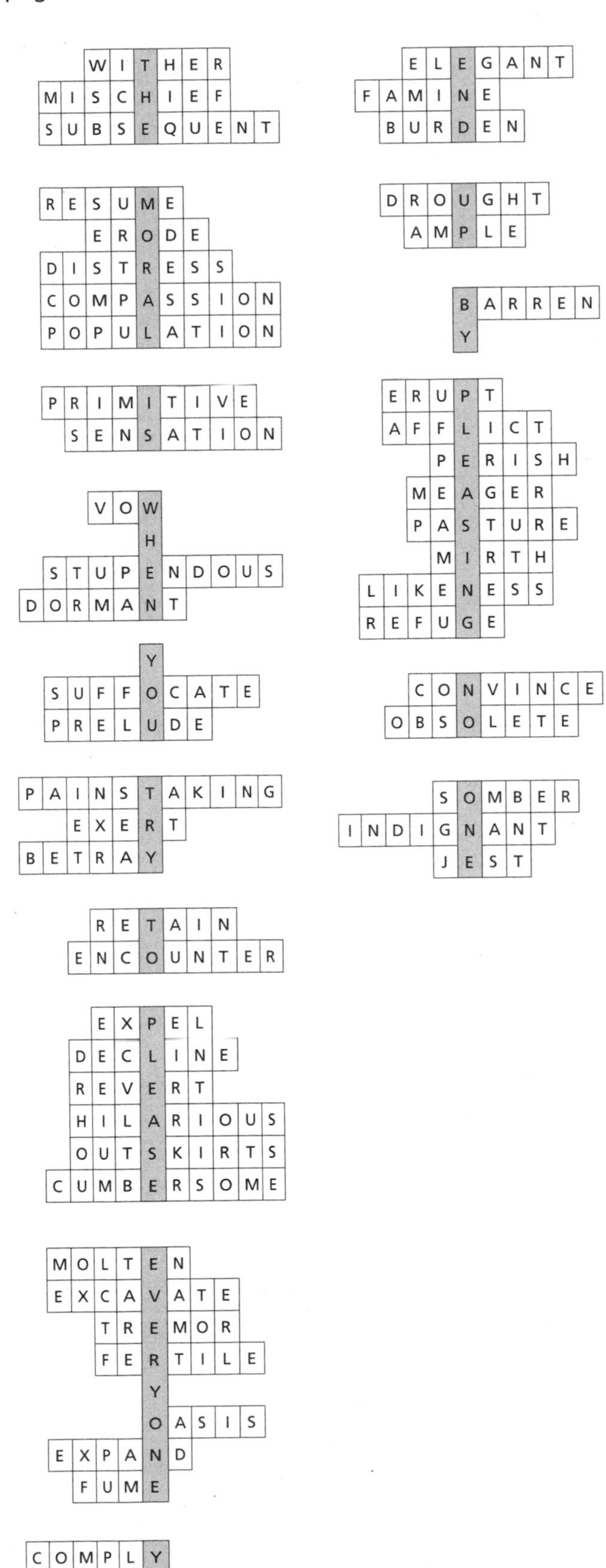

Lesson Review Exercises

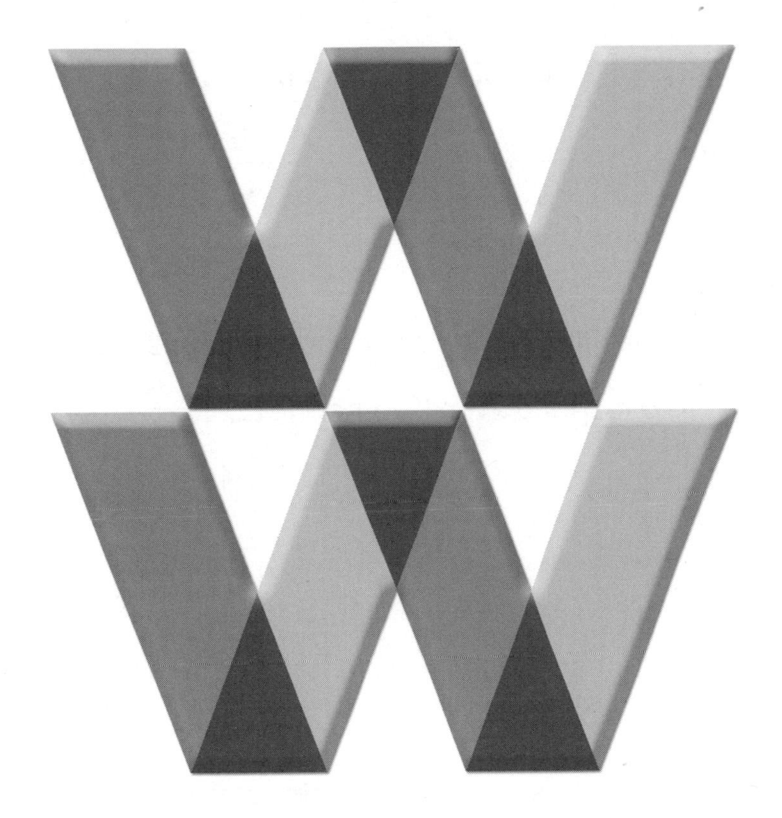

Name ______________________________ Date ______________

Review Exercise

1. Until a hundred years ago, blind people had difficulty getting around. It was at that time that someone first thought of the ______________ of guide dogs.

2. Dogs naturally like to be active and on the move. Seeing Eye dogs learn ______________ by being made to sit without moving for long periods.

3. Seeing Eye dogs must keep their minds on the job they have to do. Loud noises and interesting smells are two of the ______________ they are taught to ignore.

4. Many dogs will snap back if someone accidentally bumps into them. Guide dogs are trained not to respond even if someone ______________ them quite hard.

5. Seeing Eye dogs and their owners enjoy each other's company. They are ______________ for each other and are hardly ever separated.

6. It takes a month of getting to know one another for each dog and its future owner. At the end of that time, the dog is ______________ to its new owner.

7. Each dog is carefully matched with its new owner. A small person would not receive a large dog, which might be more suitable for a ______________ person.

8. There are many things to be considered in matching dog to owner. The most important is whether the dog and its new owner are ______________.

Review Exercise *continued*

9. Seeing Eye dogs must be able to think for themselves. Although usually ________________, they will refuse to obey an order to go forward if to do so might be dangerous.

10. Sometimes the owner tells the guide dog to cross a street where the traffic could be a danger. The dog will disobey the order and refuse to ________________ until it's safe to do so.

11. The guide dogs must be especially watchful on busy sidewalks, because ________________ don't always look where they are going.

12. If the guide dog senses danger it will refuse to go forward. It will ________________ its owner to the danger, probably by barking loudly.

13. Seeing Eye dogs guide their owners skillfully in crowded places. Some of the ________________ they might have to avoid are fire hydrants, power line poles, or trash barrels on the sidewalk.

14. The working life of a Seeing Eye dog is about ten years. It then spends its ________________ as an ordinary family pet.

15. When it gets too old to do its job, a Seeing Eye dog is placed with another family. It probably takes some time before it gets ________________ to its new home.

Name ______________________________ Date ______________

Lesson 2 **Review Exercise**

1. Until the Spanish discovered it in the 1500s, chocolate was unknown in Europe. Until that time it was ________________ only in Central and South America by the Aztecs.

2. The Aztec word *chocolate* means "bitter drink." The word was ________________ into European languages after the Spanish conquest of Central and South America.

3. The Aztecs didn't use paper money or coins when they bought things. They paid for their ________________ with cocoa beans.

4. Instead of dollars and cents, the Aztecs priced things in cocoa beans. Ten beans were ________________ in value to one rabbit.

5. The first cocoa trees grew wild in Central and South America. Now cocoa trees are ________________ in many other parts of the world.

6. The Ivory Coast in West Africa produces nearly half of the world's cocoa crop. It ________________ over a million tons a year to countries around the world.

7. The United States is not a suitable place for growing cocoa trees. They grow best in ________________ countries.

8. Cocoa beans grow close together inside each pod. The ________________ varies in size from twenty beans to as many as forty.

Review Exercise *continued*

9. Smelling fresh cocoa beans would not help you to identify them. The beans at that stage do not have the distinctive chocolate ________________.

10. Roasting makes the shells easier to crack open. This is because the heat makes them ________________.

11. Hot chocolate is a favorite drink for people of all ages. The ________________ is especially popular in wintertime.

12. Dark chocolate has a slightly bitter taste. Those who prefer it consider milk chocolate to be rather ________________.

13. Chocolate can take several different forms. What we think of as chocolate is a ________________ of cocoa powder, cocoa butter, dried milk, and sugar.

14. Cocoa powder is an important byproduct of chocolate production. It is made by ________________ the fat from chocolate paste.

15. Some people find chocolate hard to resist. Those who have a ________________ for it sometimes call themselves "chocoholics."

Name ______________________________ Date ______________

Review Exercise

1. Dinosaurs first appeared over 200 million years ago and died out 65 million years ago. That is a ______________ of about 135 million years.

2. The world of the dinosaurs was vastly different from today's world. It is impossible to ______________ what it would have been like to live in those times.

3. The world at that time was a savage one of hunters and hunted, where ______________ creatures would have stood no chance.

4. Dinosaur skeletons are found buried in rock. It is ______________ that the bones and the rock are about the same age.

5. Most creatures living tens of millions of years ago left no trace behind. Only a small number happened to be ______________ in rocks for us to discover.

6. A twenty-foot long *Utahraptor* may seem large, but it looks small when compared with the ______________ *Tyrannosaurus Rex,* which measured fifty feet.

7. Its ten-inch claws and huge, sharp teeth give *Tyrannosaurus Rex* a scary look. It is probably the most ______________ looking of all the dinosaurs.

8. Dinosaur teeth tell scientists what kind of creature the teeth belonged to. They show whether the creature was plant-eating or ______________.

Review Exercise *continued*

9. The largest of all dinosaurs ate only plants. They were not equipped to fight and were the natural ______________ of meat-eaters such as *Tyrannosaurus Rex.*

10. Did a meteorite hitting Earth cause the dinosaurs to die out? Scientists who once thought this explanation ______________ now believe it to be correct.

11. A large meteorite could hit Earth again. The damage to our planet if that were to happen would be enormous, but life in some form would almost certainly ______________.

12. Perhaps dinosaurs never died out at all but eventually became today's birds. People have the ______________ of believing either explanation.

13. Those who believe that dinosaurs never died out at all point to *Sinornis.* They think that feathered dinosaurs are the ______________ of birds living today.

14. Is there a connection between feathered dinosaurs like *Sinornis* and today's birds? The relationship between them is still ______________.

15. It may well turn out to be the case that birds are descended from dinosaurs. If that is so, then dinosaurs never really became ______________.

Name ______________________________ Date ______________

Lesson 4 Review Exercise

1. The Pilgrims who boarded the *Mayflower* left for religious reasons. They ______________ of ever being able to practice their faith in England.

2. The Pilgrims wished to be free to practice their own religion in America. They ______________ all religious ties with England when they left.

3. A hundred and two passengers boarded the *Mayflower.* When they ______________ from England, they had little hope of ever seeing their native land again.

4. The *Mayflower* left Plymouth on September 6, 1620. Its ______________ was supposed to take it to Virginia.

5. Sailors in the 1600s steered mainly by the sun and stars. In those days it was impossible for them to know their position ______________.

6. Clocks and other instruments were not very reliable in the 1600s. At best they could tell those on board only ______________ where their ship was on the ocean.

7. Sailors knew their location when they were in sight of land. To ______________ across three thousand miles of open ocean using unreliable instruments was very difficult.

8. The passengers on the *Mayflower* set off with high hopes. Their spirits ____________________ as weeks went by without sight of land.

9. After several weeks of fine weather, conditions changed. Strong ____________________ in the mid-Atlantic carried the *Mayflower* north, away from Virginia.

10. The *Mayflower* was lucky to reach America, as shipwrecks were common in the 1600s. Not all ____________________ ended successfully.

11. There was a burial at sea when one of the passengers died. The person got sick and could not be ____________________.

12. Those on board had almost given up hope of reaching America. Then, after sixty-five days, land was spotted on the ____________________.

13. The speck of land grew larger as the *Mayflower* approached Cape Cod. As the ship drew closer to the shore, the ____________________ on board increased.

14. The *Mayflower* was supposed to land in Virginia. Its actual ____________________ turned out to be five hundred miles to the north.

15. The Pilgrims took a few personal belongings with them. Looking at them in their new land must have made them feel ____________________.

Name ________________________________ Date ______________

Lesson 5

Review Exercise

1. What is it that attracts men and women to risk their lives climbing Everest? The ________________ of the mountain is hard to explain to nonclimbers.

2. Perhaps George Mallory thought it foolish for someone to ask him why he wanted to climb Everest. That might explain his ________________ reply, "Because it's there."

3. Mallory made several unsuccessful attempts to climb Everest. The ________________ was not just to reach the top, but to be the first to do so.

4. Mallory's final climb up Everest took place in 1924 and ended with his death. Several ________________ attempts had also ended in failure.

5. Thousands of people have tried to climb Everest. The mountain's extreme weather ________________ the attempt by five out of six climbers.

6. Nervous people would not enjoy mountain climbing. Looking down a thousand-foot ________________ mountain face while dangling from a rope can be especially scary.

7. The height of Everest has been carefully measured. Its ________________ is twenty-nine thousand and thirty-five feet above sea level.

8. There are several ways to climb Everest. Most climbers take the ________________ up the south side of the mountain.

Review Exercise *continued*

9. Climbers must train hard before attempting to climb Everest. To try to make it to the top while in poor physical condition would be ____________________.

10. The weather on the higher parts of the mountain changes with very little warning. When bad weather suddenly strikes, ____________________ can turn to despair.

11. A mass of ice, snow, and rocks can become dislodged near the peak. The ____________________ gathers speed as it roars down the mountain.

12. Climbers must seek shelter from strong winds and falling snow. A ____________________ on Mount Everest can last for hours or even days.

13. Climbers make their way very carefully up steep slopes. As they climb up, they look for ____________________ to use as hand- or footholds.

14. Most climbers carry sturdy but lightweight tents. Having a tent makes having to rely on ____________________ shelters unnecessary.

15. Most climbers of tall mountains admit to being afraid at times. They say that one of the benefits of climbing is learning to ____________________ fear.

Name ______________________________ Date ______________

Lesson 6

Review Exercise

1. The years leading up to the Civil War were marked by strong disagreements. Tension ________________ between North and South until war broke out.

2. Those who helped slaves escaping from their owners put themselves at risk. It was a crime to ________________ runaway slaves.

3. Stowe felt that she had to do something to help end slavery. She wrote *Uncle Tom's Cabin* to ________________ the people against what she felt was a terrible evil.

4. Slaveholders could break up whole families by selling their members separately. We cannot imagine the ________________ suffered by the parents and their children.

5. There are some hateful people in *Uncle Tom's Cabin*. Readers of the book probably feel the greatest ________________ for Simon Legree.

6. Legree treated Uncle Tom brutally. Trying to make him whip the weak, female slave was a ________________ act.

7. Punishment was harsh for slaves who displeased their masters. The whipping ________________ on Uncle Tom was so severe that he died.

8. Eliza and her child are central to the story of *Uncle Tom's Cabin*. These are the two ________________ that readers probably care about the most.

Review Exercise *continued*

9. Eliza made up her mind to escape. She made her decision after hearing the ____________________ news that her child was to be sold.

10. Southern slave owners were upset by *Uncle Tom's Cabin.* They ____________________ Stowe for interfering in matters she didn't understand.

11. Supporters of the South told Stowe to mind her own business and stay out of theirs. She would probably have replied that she was proud to be called ____________________.

12. Stowe devoted her life to ending slavery. It must have made her very happy when slavery was ____________________ in 1863 by order of President Lincoln.

13. Stowe wrote other books besides *Uncle Tom's Cabin.* It was her story of slavery in America that ____________________ her to world fame.

14. *Uncle Tom's Cabin* was popular with readers all over the world. It was first ____________________ into German and then into many other languages.

15. Harriet Beecher Stowe shows that one person can make a difference. She was ____________________ in her determination to end slavery.

Name ______________________ Date ____________

Lesson 7

Review Exercise

1. Penguins are a popular feature of many aquariums. These ______________ creatures always draw crowds of onlookers.

2. Gentlemen put on evening clothes only for special occasions. Penguins appear in "______________" dress all the time.

3. There are differences in appearance between one penguin and another. To a casual onlooker, however, they all ______________ each other.

4. Antarctica, where penguins make their home, is not an easy place to get to. It is in a very ______________ part of the world.

5. Antarctica is the coldest place on Earth. The ______________ air during the long winter night can measure negative seventy degrees.

6. Penguins are able to survive in the ______________ climate.

7. Penguins need the company of other penguins in order to survive the extreme cold. That is why they live in large ______________.

8. Penguins have learned to get along with each other. This is just as well, as up to half a million may be ______________ together in one place.

Review Exercise *continued*

9. There's an old saying that birds of a feather flock together. That's true of these birds of Antarctica, as a ________________ penguin would be a very rare sight.

10. All birds lay eggs. Most do so in nests of twigs and grass, but female penguins ________________ their eggs in nests made of stones.

11. Young penguin chicks have food brought to them by their parents. They are too ________________ to survive on their own.

12. Penguins need lots of food in order to stay alive. A ________________ part of their day is spent in the water hunting for fish.

13. Penguins long ago lost the ability to fly. They ________________ for this by being excellent swimmers.

14. Flexible wings would not make good flippers for moving through water. The penguin's ________________ wings enable it to move quickly in the sea.

15. Penguins seem more at home in water than on land. On land they ________________ awkwardly, but they move gracefully in the water.

Name ______________________________ Date ________________

Review Exercise

1. Thanksgiving is a popular holiday in the United States. It is ________________ each year on the fourth Thursday in November.

2. Thanksgiving brings families together around the dinner table. The centerpiece of the ________________ is usually a roast turkey.

3. The first Thanksgiving was held in late 1621. At that time the Pilgrims gave thanks for their first ________________.

4. Forty-one passengers had met the previous year in the *Mayflower's* main cabin. At that ________________, they drew up the rules by which they would govern themselves.

5. The set of rules was known as the Mayflower Compact. All those who signed it ________________ to observe the agreement.

6. The *Mayflower* carried everything the Pilgrims would need in the New World. Musical instruments, considered unimportant, were not part of the ________________.

7. Liquids were brought over on the *Mayflower* in watertight barrels. These ________________ could later be used by the Pilgrims to store water.

8. Axes were very important tools. With them the Pilgrims could ________________ logs from the forest trees to make their homes.

Review Exercise *continued*

9. Everyone who was able to had to work. Small children might be given the ________________ of collecting firewood.

10. The Pilgrims were starving by the end of the winter. When Samoset visited them, their supplies of food had ________________ to almost nothing.

11. By early 1621, many had died and most of the others were sick. Just when things were most ________________, help arrived.

12. The Pilgrims were too feeble to defend themselves if attacked. Luckily the Wampanoags were not ________________.

13. It was important for the Pilgrims to know which berries could be eaten safely. The Wampanoags showed them which were ________________ and which were poisonous.

14. Other ships followed the *Mayflower,* bringing more goods and people from England. The Plymouth colony became quite ________________ as trade with England grew.

15. The Pilgrims took life very seriously. If they could come back today, they would probably think that most Americans lead very ________________ lives.

Name ______________________________ Date ______________

Lesson 9 Review Exercise

1. The air inside a hot-air balloon is heated. This makes it less ______________ than the surrounding cooler air and causes the balloon to rise.

2. In 1783 a large crowd assembled to watch the Montgolfier brothers' hot-air balloon. Among the ______________ were members of the French royal family.

3. The Montgolfier brothers' hot-air balloon reached a height of 1,500 feet. Its flight ______________ after it had been in the air for eight minutes.

4. Unlike a kite, the Montgolfier brothers' hot-air balloon was not attached to the ground. People watched in amazement as the balloon ______________ to a great height.

5. A sheep, a duck, and a rooster were the first airborne creatures. Two months later, the first human flight in a balloon took place, a truly ______________ act.

6. By 1900, there was great competition to build a successful heavier-than-air flying machine. The first to ______________ this goal would be famous.

7. The Wright brothers made and repaired bicycles for a living. They ______________ their work on bicycles to concentrate on building a heavier-than-air flying machine.

8. Some early aircraft had as many as six wings, stacked above each other. Such airplanes were too ______________ to ever get off the ground.

Review Exercise *continued*

9. Modern aircraft have rigid wings. Early attempts to ________________ the flapping of birds' wings ended in failure.

10. The first aircraft designers had a problem in trying to reduce the plane's weight. The lighter the aircraft, the more ________________ it was.

11. Steam engines are very heavy. It was ________________ to think they could ever be used to power aircraft.

12. The Wright brothers rejected the concept of steam-powered flight. After ________________ with different designs, they developed a lightweight gasoline engine.

13. The first flying machine took to the air in 1903. Only a few people were present to see the plane ________________ to a height of a few feet and stay in the air for twelve seconds.

14. The future ________________ of aircraft may not have been obvious to everyone. They might have been surprised to hear that one day aircraft would be flown around the world and even into space.

15. A visit to the National Air and Space Museum is a must in Washington, D.C. There you can see the plane that ________________ across the field at Kitty Hawk and then took off.

Name ______________________________ Date ______________

Review Exercise

1. Slavery had many defenders in the Congress of the 1850s. They based their attitude on the belief that the white race was ______________ to all others.

2. Many slave owners claimed that their slaves were happy. The truth was that every slave ______________ to be free.

3. White slave owners thought there was nothing wrong in owning slaves. They argued that people had been living in ______________ for thousands of years.

4. There was once some uncertainty regarding the year of Harriet Tubman's birth. It has now been ______________ that she was born in 1820.

5. Harriet Tubman wanted desperately to free as many slaves as possible. She ______________ her goal with a single-minded purpose.

6. The former slave had wealthy friends who wanted to help her. They made money ______________ to her whenever she needed it.

7. The money Tubman earned at various jobs paid for her own living expenses. To do her real work she relied on ______________ from her supporters.

8. She returned to the South many times to help others escape. There were ______________ times when she was almost captured by reward hunters.

Review Exercise *continued*

9. The $40,000 reward for capturing her was a lure for those who hunted Tubman. No one ever received the reward as she always ________________ capture.

10. The Fugitive Slave Law was passed by Congress in 1850. It ________________ anyone from helping a runaway slave.

11. It took courage to belong to the Underground Railroad. The law against helping runaway slaves made most people ________________ to help Tubman and others like her.

12. The Civil War tore apart many families. Brothers sometimes ________________ brothers, and fathers fought against sons.

13. Tubman made many trips behind enemy lines. On these ________________ she tried to win slaves over to the Northern side.

14. Slaves were taught to fear the Northern soldiers. Tubman won their trust and was able to offer them ________________ that they accepted.

15. The year1863 has great significance in American history. In that year, President Lincoln signed an order ________________ all the slaves in the states fighting the North.

Name ______________________________ Date ______________

Lesson 11 **Review Exercise**

1. Poems have been written about the joy of flying. They try to capture the ______________ feeling that comes from soaring far above the earth.

2. Flying an airplane alone for the first time is an unforgettable experience. Pilots never forget their first ______________ flight.

3. Many people are afraid of flying, especially going up for the first time. The more times you fly, the less ______________ you become.

4. All student pilots are nervous when flying alone for the first time. No matter how ______________ they try to seem, their hearts are beating a little more rapidly.

5. The way you walk tells something of how you feel. By ______________ rather than hurrying, you give the impression that you aren't worried.

6. Instructor and student pilot should be compatible. It's important that they have ______________ in each other.

7. Pilots go through a series of steps before takeoff. They ______________ from each item on the checklist to the next until all have been checked off.

8. Pilots do everything in a careful manner. By acting ______________ at all times, they avoid making mistakes that could be fatal.

Review Exercise *continued*

9. Pilots must be alert for instructions from the ground. They remain in radio ________________ with the tower at all times.

10. Opening the throttle makes the engine turn faster. This causes the plane to ________________ until it reaches its takeoff speed.

11. An altimeter is an instrument that shows how high the plane is. It measures air pressure and gives the ________________ of the plane above sea level.

12. A plane burns the least amount of gas at its cruising speed. It consumes much more fuel when flying at ________________ speed.

13. To land, the pilot closes the throttle and pulls back on the stick when the plane is just inches off the ground. This causes the plane to ________________ and drop gently onto the runway.

14. Landing a plane can be tricky and even dangerous. Pilots ________________ themselves before landing in case they have to act quickly in an emergency.

15. Aircraft are usually parked on the airport tarmac. They are wheeled into the ________________ for overhauls and repairs.

Name ______________________________ Date ______________

Review Exercise

1. Frida Kahlo was born in Mexico in 1907 during the rule of Porfirio Diaz. At that time Mexican women stayed home and were ______________ from public life.

2. Even as a child, Frida found it hard to take orders from others. She remained a ______________ all her life, not always doing what was expected.

3. The young girl must have been the despair of her parents. She would not allow them, or anyone else, to ______________ to her what she must do.

4. Following the revolution, hospitals and schools were improved, and government support for the arts greatly increased. These changes were long ______________.

5. Kahlo called herself a child of the revolution. She wanted people to believe she had been born in 1910, the year the Diaz government was ______________.

6. The young Frida had two great passions. She ______________ her life to art and to the aims of the 1910 revolution.

7. Kahlo's parents must have been horrified when their daughter expressed support for the revolution. That was no way for a girl with a strict Catholic ______________ to behave.

8. Her wearing men's clothing must have been especially shocking to Frida's parents. Such a sight was ______________ seen in Mexico at that time.

Review Exercise *continued*

9. In her late teens, Kahlo had a terrible accident. A metal spike ____________________ her side when she was thrown from a bus.

10. She was often in agony from the injury. To take her mind off the pain while she ____________________, she started painting.

11. The first marriage between Kahlo and Rivera took place in 1929. She was quite unknown at the time, while he was one of Mexico's most ____________________ painters.

12. Rivera appears often in Kahlo's paintings. Perhaps she found him so fascinating because he loved and ____________________ her at the same time.

13. Kahlo painted Rivera many times. She also frequently portrayed herself, and many of her paintings are self-____________________.

14. Kahlo and Rivera had a love-hate relationship. Each ____________________ quarrel would be short-lived but then would be followed by another one.

15. Kahlo and Rivera found in each other something that made their work come alive. They ____________________ each other's passion for both life and art.

Name ______________________________ Date ______________

Lesson 13 **Review Exercise**

1. Different animals have different ways of moving on land. Frogs hop and penguins waddle, while crocodiles ______________ when they leave the water.

2. Animals' tails, too, come in all shapes and sizes. A beaver's tail is spadelike, while that of a crocodile ______________ to a point.

3. Crocodiles and alligators are similar in many respects. One difference is that the fourth tooth of a crocodile can be seen sticking out from its ______________.

4. Crocodiles, like all reptiles, are cold-blooded. They are more active when it's warm and become ______________ when the temperature drops.

5. To cool off, the crocodile digs a hole in the soft ground. It makes the hole large enough to ______________ its whole body.

6. A well-fed crocodile is not likely to be dangerous. How ______________ it is depends on how long it has been since its last meal.

7. Crocodiles hunt their prey from the water. A crocodile ______________ on land is unlikely to attack something or someone.

8. A crocodile under water is hard to see. Only its eyes and nostrils ______________ above the surface of the river or lake.

Review Exercise *continued*

9. The crocodile moves to the attack without disturbing the surface of the water. Even a small ________________ would scare away its prey.

10. The crocodile is able to swim closer and closer without being seen. It only becomes ________________ when it leaps out of the water to attack.

11. Crocodiles eat almost anything. A fresh piece of meat or a week-old ________________ is equally tasty to a hungry croc.

12. Sometimes a crocodile kills an animal too large for a single meal. It takes what it cannot eat and ________________ it in a place to which it can later return.

13. Smaller crocodiles are sometimes eaten by larger ones. Spotting a bite-sized baby croc, all the big croc sees is a tasty ________________.

14. A croc has two powerful weapons to use against its prey. It can bite with its jaws and it can ________________ with its powerful tail.

15. Unlike its host, the crocodile bird doesn't have to hunt for food. It flies into the croc's mouth and ________________ on the scraps of meat stuck between its teeth.

Name ______________________________ Date ______________

Review Exercise

1. Edison's childhood was in some ways a solitary one. The other children at his school would not ____________ with him.

2. The young Edison withdrew from his schoolmates. He was quiet and thoughtful, while they were ____________ and unkind to him.

3. Edison showed from an early age that he was very strong-minded. He probably did not allow the ____________ of his classmates to upset him too much.

4. Edison never claimed to be a city boy. In fact, much of Michigan where he grew up was still ____________.

5. Edison was granted over a thousand patents. Money received from these patents ____________ him with the funds to continue his research.

6. Two things made it possible for Edison to do so much. During his waking hours he was never ____________, and he needed less sleep than most people.

7. Edison didn't believe in wasting time. He ____________ almost every waking moment working on or improving new inventions.

8. He was strict in his dealings with others. He would not ____________ laziness in himself or others.

9. The electric light bulb was probably Edison's most useful invention. Light was instantly ____________________ with the flick of a switch.

10. Edison's light bulb was made of clear glass. Inside it a ____________________ thread began to glow when electricity passed through it.

11. Edison tried many kinds of thread before finding one that worked. Such an effort on his part ____________________ great patience.

12. The concept of electric light spread rapidly. Within a few years, whole cities were being ____________________ by electricity.

13. Electric power soon became widely available in the United States. This brought about a total ____________________ in people's lives.

14. Edison never really retired. He continued working until he died in 1931, in the ninth ____________________ of his long and busy life.

15. Edison's place in history is secure. He was without doubt the most ____________________ inventor of the nineteenth century.

Name ______________________ Date ____________

Lesson 15 Review Exercise

1. Hurricanes, tornadoes, floods and forest fires all do great damage. The greatest of all natural ______________, however, are earthquakes.

2. Earthquakes do most damage because they strike without warning. With a hurricane, people usually have enough time to ______________ to safety.

3. Those who have lived through a big earthquake never forget it. Once you have felt the ground ______________ beneath your feet, the earth never feels quite the same afterward.

4. The worst earthquake ever recorded happened in China in 1556. The damage was ______________, and almost a million people died.

5. The 1906 San Francisco earthquake started a terrible fire and killed 450 people. Those who survived it must have been ______________ until the danger passed.

6. Buildings need not collapse even in a large earthquake. Walls can be strengthened to keep them from ______________.

7. The location of an earthquake makes a difference to what happens. The more ______________ settled an area is, the less chance there is of serious damage.

8. Cities built on one of the earth's faults are most at risk. In recent decades, large ______________ areas like San Francisco and Los Angeles have been hit hard.

Review Exercise *continued*

9. Faults in the earth's crust run through areas bordering the Pacific Ocean. These areas are ____________________ to earthquakes.

10. The San Andreas Fault runs six hundred miles along California. It lies on a ____________________ in the earth's crust that causes seismologists to worry.

11. Seismologists are scientists who study earthquakes. The more they learn about them, the better they hope to become at ____________________ when one will occur.

12. Seismologists track earthquakes wherever they occur. Each one is ____________________ carefully in the hope of learning more about what causes these events.

13. The Richter scale measures the strength of earthquakes. The higher the number, the more ____________________ the earthquake.

14. One number higher on the scale means a tenfold increase in strength. A ____________________ earthquake that measures 8.0 packs ten times the punch of one rated 7.0.

15. A higher Richter number may not mean more damage or deaths. Even a ____________________ earthquake can do damage if buildings are too flimsy to withstand the shock.

Name ______________________ Date ____________

Review Exercise

1. Liliuokalani and Kalakaua occupied a high position in Hawaiian society. They counted the Hawaiian royal family among their ________________.

2. King Lunalilo ruled for just one year. Following his death, Kalakaua ________________ the position of ruler.

3. Kalakaua was an unexpected choice by Hawaii's governing body. As the widow of the ________________ king, Queen Emma had been expected to succeed him as the new ruler.

4. Kalakaua found himself under pressure from the *haoles*, the white planters from the United States. He gradually ________________ his powers and became ruler in name only.

5. In 1887 the whole world celebrated Queen Victoria's fifty years on the English throne. Kalakaua sent his sister to attend the Golden ________________.

6. Liliuokalani's rule as queen followed her brother's death in 1891. She ________________ for just two years until forced to step aside in 1893.

7. In 1893, a committee of *haoles* met to decide Hawaii's future. It ________________ Sanford Dole president of the new Republic of Hawaii.

8. The native Hawaiians felt helpless as they slowly lost control of the islands. The government of Hawaii became increasingly ________________ by the *haoles*.

Review Exercise *continued*

9. The native Hawaiians disliked the government imposed on them by the *haoles*. The attempt to overthrow it was ________________, and the rebels were thrown in prison.

10. Resentment against the *haoles* grew stronger. The native Hawaiians were ________________ into rebelling because they were losing control of their government.

11. Sanford Dole was looking for a reason to break the resistance of Liliuokalani's followers. He may have used the ________________ that broke out as an excuse to interfere.

12. Liliuokalani was believed to be closely associated with the rebels. Messages from her to them that were ________________ seemed to bear this out.

13. Liliuokalani believed she had to stand up to the *haoles*. She regarded herself as the ________________ of traditional Hawaiian values.

14. During World War One, Liliuokalani raised the Stars and Stripes for the first time. This showed that she had ________________ the United States for taking away her country.

15. The immediate cause of her action was the death of the first Hawaiian soldier in the war. She ________________ the American flag as a gesture of goodwill.

Name ______________________________ Date ______________

Lesson 17 Review Exercise

1. Africa is the second-largest continent, after Asia. It ______________ of over fifty countries, and its people speak over a thousand different languages.

2. The world's largest desert, the Sahara, is in Africa. Travelers across it make their way from one ______________ to the next, spending a night at each as they proceed on their way.

3. The continent has suffered greatly because of both natural and man-made disasters. Hunger, disease, and war are three of Africa's greatest ______________ .

4. Some countries in Africa are quite prosperous. If the country is at peace and the soil is ______________, life can be good in these countries.

5. Climate changes greatly affect what happens to the land. Desert may ______________ to grassland in one part of the continent, and the opposite may occur somewhere else.

6. Cattle are a measure of wealth in many parts of Africa. A loss of ______________ means the size of the herd must be reduced.

7. Farmers in sub-Saharan Africa keep a close eye on the weather. Lots of rain means a good harvest, while little or no rain means the crops will ______________ and die.

8. Farmers are helpless as they watch their crops fail for lack of water. No longer able to survive on the ________________ land, the people move to the cities.

9. Some periods without rain last for a few weeks, while others go on for years. There is no way to predict when a ________________ will end.

10. Cutting down trees can be harmful for the land. Tree roots hold the soil in place and prevent it from being ________________ by heavy rains.

11. Makeshift camps are set up to house people fleeing the advancing desert. These camps are ________________ with people who have little hope for the future.

12. Babies born in these camps can expect to live there all their lives. Housing, education, and health services, if they are available at all, are often extremely ________________ .

13. The people forced to leave home would like nothing better than for conditions to improve so that they can return to their farms. They are not ________________ by choice.

14. Food for the starving people arrives at African ports. For a variety of reasons, it often fails to reach the victims of ________________ .

15. Ending world hunger is a challenge for rich countries. They will need to ________________ their efforts if they are to succeed.

Name ______________________ Date ____________

Review Exercise

1. Disney started out with no money. He ______________ his uncle to lend him five hundred dollars to start his company.

2. Disney's early years in the film business were not easy. At first he could afford to pay himself only enough for a ______________ living.

3. Oswald, the Lucky Rabbit, was one of Disney's early creations. Mickey Mouse was ______________ to Oswald, as were the rest of the famous Disney characters.

4. The distributor handling Disney's movies tried to cheat him. The distributor even lured away the illustrators Disney had ______________ earlier.

5. Disney was dismayed by the distributor's underhanded ways. He felt ______________ and decided that in the future, he would control every part of the business himself.

6. On the journey back to Los Angeles, Disney made a decision. He ______________ never to sell his movies, but only to rent them from that point on.

7. By renting his films, Disney made life easier for himself. Distributors had fewer chances to make ______________ for him if he kept ownership of the films.

8. Disney and his wife were both excited by the idea of a cartoon mouse. They had a very ______________ discussion about it on the train journey home.

Review Exercise *continued*

9. They named the new character Mickey Mouse. Mickey always seems to be happy and smiling, and it's hard to imagine him looking ________________ .

10. Mickey Mouse is always getting into and out of trouble. He ________________ his way around all obstacles with a smile on his face.

11. The only things Mickey Mouse and a real mouse have in common are that both have a tail and big ears. The ________________ between a real mouse and Disney's creation is slight.

12. Mickey Mouse was soon joined by Minnie Mouse, Goofy, and Donald Duck. These ________________ characters appeared together in many movies.

13. The first full-length talking picture appeared in 1927. Silent movies ________________ rapidly in popularity with the arrival of talking pictures.

14. The name of the first talking picture was *The Jazz Singer*. The movie created a ________________ when Al Jolson's voice rang out from the screen.

15. The arrival of sound had made silent movies ________________ overnight. Disney added a soundtrack to the third Mickey Mouse cartoon, *Steamboat Willie*.

Name ______________________ Date ____________

Review Exercise

1. Pompeii was located about a hundred and thirty miles south of Rome. It was ____________ by Romans who preferred life in a small town to that of the great city of Rome.

2. About twenty thousand people lived in this prosperous port city. It had many ____________ public buildings and private homes.

3. Pompeii was nestled under Mount Vesuvius. The four-thousand-foot mountain was actually a volcano that had been ____________ for eight hundred years.

4. The people of Pompeii had no reason to fear the mountain. Even had they known it was a volcano, they would have thought the chance of an ____________ very small.

5. Over the centuries, enormous pressure built up inside the volcano. These ____________ forces shook the earth in the 62 C.E. earthquake.

6. The earthquake should have served as a warning. The townspeople felt the ____________ from it but failed to connect the earthquake with the mountain towering over them.

7. The earthquake damaged some buildings, which were quickly repaired. But the earthquake was actually the ____________ to something far worse.

Review Exercise *continued*

8. The top of the volcano gave no clue as to what lay beneath. Long before, __________________ rock had hardened to form a plug that acted like a cork in a fizzy bottle.

9. Far from declining after the earthquake, the pressure increased. In 79 C.E., the plug was __________________ in a tremendous explosion that released the built-up pressure.

10. What had seemed like heaven turned into a hell on Earth. The air was filled with poisonous __________________ as hot lava, ash, and even boulders rained down.

11. The townspeople had no time to escape. Many were __________________ by the thick smoke and died on the spot.

12. Boiling water was forced up through cracks in the ground. People and animals were __________________ as they tried to flee the town.

13. It is impossible to get an accurate count of how many died in Pompeii. The number of those who __________________ was measured not in the hundreds but in the thousands.

14. Pompeii has much to teach us about life in the Roman Empire. Much of what we know comes from __________________ that were first begun in 1763.

15. Digging into the past continues to this day at Pompeii. The work is slow and __________________, but very rewarding when a major discovery is made.

Name ______________________________ Date ______________

Lesson 20 Review Exercise

1. A fable is a special kind of story. It makes us laugh, but it is intended to do more than just provoke ______________ in the reader.

2. A fable often has a serious purpose. The ones told by Aesop have a ______________ that teaches a lesson about life.

3. "A Tale of Two Donkeys" is a good example of a fable. It tells of a series of ______________ between a farmer and his daughter and people they meet.

4. The story pokes fun at the father. He is shown as a rather ______________ person with no mind of his own.

5. The farmer's problem is that he is so anxious to please everyone he meets. He ______________ with every suggestion made to him, no matter how unreasonable it is.

6. The pair make several stops on the way to the market. Each time, they change their positions before ______________ their journey.

7. The two start out with the farmer riding the donkey. The woman at the well feels ______________ for the daughter and scolds the father for riding while she walks.

8. Things get crowded when both try to ride the donkey, as the young man suggests. While there is ______________ room for one person, the donkey barely has room for two.

9. Carrying one person is easy for the donkey. Putting an extra person on the animal adds to its ________________ .

10. A woman they meet later is upset by what she sees. Her ________________ is aroused at the sight of two people riding one donkey.

11. The woman tells the farmer that he and his daughter should be carrying the donkey instead. He takes her ________________ seriously and ties the donkey's legs to a pole.

12. The sight of the farmer and his daughter carrying the donkey must have been hilarious. To carry such a ________________ load must have been very difficult.

13. The most difficult part of the journey was when both were carrying the donkey. They were forced to ________________ themselves in order to hold so much weight.

14. The farmer and his daughter staggered along the road toward the market. They knew they were near their destination when they reached the ________________ of the town.

15. The story doesn't tell us what the daughter thought of her father's actions. We know she was obedient, but was she ________________ by her father's foolish behavior?

Lesson Review Answer Key

Lesson 1

1. concept
2. patience
3. distractions
4. jostles
5. companions
6. assigned
7. burly
8. compatible
9. obedient
10. budge
11. pedestrians
12. alert
13. obstacles
14. retirement
15. accustomed

Lesson 2

1. consumed
2. introduced
3. purchases
4. equivalent
5. cultivated
6. exports
7. tropical
8. cluster
9. aroma
10. brittle
11. beverage
12. bland
13. combination
14. extracting
15. craving

Lesson 3

1. duration
2. comprehend
3. puny
4. evident
5. preserved
6. gigantic
7. ferocious
8. carnivorous
9. prey
10. premature
11. survive
12. option
13. ancestors
14. obscure
15. extinct

Lesson 4

1. despaired
2. severed
3. departed
4. course
5. accurately
6. approximately
7. navigate
8. deteriorated
9. gales
10. voyages
11. revived
12. horizon
13. jubilation
14. destination
15. nostalgic

Lesson 5

1. lure
2. terse
3. challenge
4. previous
5. thwarts
6. vertical
7. summit
8. route
9. foolhardy
10. optimism
11. avalanche
12. blizzard
13. crevices
14. makeshift
15. conquer

Lesson 6

1. escalated
2. harbor
3. rouse
4. agony
5. loathing
6. monstrous
7. inflicted
8. characters
9. grim
10. denounced
11. meddlesome
12. abolished
13. catapulted
14. translated
15. steadfast

Lesson 7

1. fascinating
2. formal
3. resemble
4. remote
5. frigid
6. harsh
7. colonies
8. huddled
9. solitary
10. deposit
11. feeble
12. substantial
13. compensated
14. rigid
15. waddle

Lesson 8

1. celebrated
2. banquet
3. harvest
4. assembly
5. pledged
6. cargo
7. casks
8. hew
9. task
10. decreased
11. desperate
12. hostile
13. edible
14. prosperous
15. frivolous

Lesson 9

1. dense
2. spectators
3. terminated
4. soared
5. heroic
6. accomplish
7. suspended
8. unwieldy
9. mimic
10. flimsy
11. absurd
12. experimenting
13. ascend
14. significance
15. lumbered

Lesson 10

1. superior
2. yearned
3. bondage
4. established
5. pursued
6. available
7. donations
8. numerous
9. evaded
10. prohibited
11. reluctant
12. opposed
13. occasions
14. reassurances
15. liberating

Lesson 11

1. exultant
2. solo
3. anxious
4. nonchalant
5. sauntering
6. confidence
7. proceed
8. methodically
9. contact
10. accelerate
11. altitude
12. maximum
13. stall
14. brace
15. hangar

Lesson 12

1. restricted
2. rebel
3. dictate
4. overdue
5. overthrown
6. dedicated
7. upbringing
8. seldom
9. penetrated
10. convalesced
11. notable
12. exasperated
13. portraits
14. tempestuous
15. stimulated

Lesson 13

1. slither
2. tapers
3. snout
4. sluggish
5. accommodate
6. aggressive
7. basking
8. protrude
9. ripple
10. visible
11. carcass
12. conceals
13. morsel
14. flail
15. gorges

Lesson 14

1. associate
2. boisterous
3. taunts
4. wilderness
5. provided
6. idle
7. employed
8. tolerate
9. accessible
10. delicate
11. required
12. illuminated
13. transformation
14. decade
15. brilliant

Lesson 15

1. disasters
2. flee
3. lurch
4. immense
5. petrified
6. toppling
7. sparsely
8. urban
9. prone
10. fracture
11. predicting
12. investigated
13. intense
14. major
15. minor

Lesson 16

1. kin
2. assumed
3. former
4. abdicated
5. Jubilee
6. reigned
7. proclaimed
8. dominated
9. bungled
10. provoked
11. riot
12. intercepted
13. guardian
14. pardoned
15. hoisted

Lesson 17

1. consists
2. oasis
3. afflictions
4. fertile
5. revert
6. pasture
7. wither
8. barren
9. drought
10. eroded
11. teeming
12. primitive
13. refugees
14. famine
15. expand

Lesson 18

1. convinced
2. meager
3. subsequent
4. retained
5. betrayed
6. vowed
7. mischief
8. animated
9. somber
10. negotiates
11. likeness
12. hilarious
13. declined
14. sensation
15. obsolete

Lesson 19

1. populated
2. elegant
3. dormant
4. eruption
5. stupendous
6. tremors
7. prelude
8. molten
9. expelled
10. fumes
11. suffocated
12. scalded
13. perished
14. excavations
15. painstaking

Lesson 20

1. mirth
2. moral
3. encounters
4. ridiculous
5. complies
6. resuming
7. compassion
8. ample
9. burden
10. indignation
11. jest
12. cumbersome
13. exert
14. outskirts
15. distressed

Book 5 Tests

Name ______________________________ Date ______________

Lesson 1 Test

Choose the best way to complete each sentence or answer each question. Then fill in the circle next to your answer.

1. When you are given a class **assignment,** you are expected to
   - Ⓐ appear at a certain time.
   - Ⓑ sit in a certain place.
   - Ⓒ complete a task.
   - Ⓓ take charge of other people.

2. A **patient** is someone who is
   - Ⓐ waiting in line at the store.
   - Ⓑ being seen by a doctor.
   - Ⓒ sitting quietly.
   - Ⓓ trying to hurry.

3. My aunt will move to Florida after she **retires.** She will move after she
   - Ⓐ changes jobs.
   - Ⓑ makes more money.
   - Ⓒ gets very old.
   - Ⓓ stops working.

4. Two men could not **budge** the sofa. This was probably because the sofa was
   - Ⓐ too heavy.
   - Ⓑ too expensive.
   - Ⓒ too old.
   - Ⓓ too likely to fall apart.

5. If your dog is **obedient,** it
   - Ⓐ is friendly to strangers.
   - Ⓑ bothers your neighbors.
   - Ⓒ does what you tell it to do.
   - Ⓓ has health problems.

6. The radio **alerted** us to the coming storm. As a result, we
   - Ⓐ did not expect the storm.
   - Ⓑ were ready for the storm.
   - Ⓒ felt relieved.
   - Ⓓ did not expect it to be serious.

7. To **accustom** yourself to life in another country, you must
   - Ⓐ get used to doing things in new ways.
   - Ⓑ introduce other people to your customs.
   - Ⓒ leave your family behind.
   - Ⓓ learn several languages.

8. I am looking for a **companion** for my trip to Mexico. Which of the following is a **companion?**

   Ⓐ a tent that I can camp in
   Ⓑ a tour group that I can join
   Ⓒ someone to travel with
   Ⓓ an inexpensive flight

9. Which could be a **concept** for a new invention?

   Ⓐ a group of important scientists
   Ⓑ a television commercial for the invention
   Ⓒ an idea for a machine that does your homework
   Ⓓ a scientific lab

10. Which of the following shows **obedience?**

    Ⓐ Students use their imaginations.
    Ⓑ Students help one another with their class work.
    Ⓒ Students are noisy.
    Ⓓ Students do what the teacher asks.

11. Kayla and her sister were not **compatible** until they were teenagers. Before they were teenagers, they probably

    Ⓐ fought a lot.
    Ⓑ were always mistaken for one another.
    Ⓒ got along well.
    Ⓓ shared everything with each other.

12. To which of the following can a student be **assigned?**

    Ⓐ his or her parents
    Ⓑ the principal's office
    Ⓒ a math group
    Ⓓ a best friend

13. We had our **accustomed** lunch of peanut butter and banana sandwiches. What does **accustomed** mean in this sentence?

    Ⓐ usual
    Ⓑ unusual
    Ⓒ stale
    Ⓓ delicious

14. Good babysitters are always **alert.** In this sentence, **alert** means

    Ⓐ watchful and wide-awake.
    Ⓑ fun and energetic.
    Ⓒ not easily upset.
    Ⓓ trained in first aid.

15. Which of the following is most likely to be **burly?**

    Ⓐ a baby
    Ⓑ a weight lifter
    Ⓒ a tulip
    Ⓓ a bicycle

16. I was **jostled** by the crowd in the subway station. I was

Ⓐ pleased.

Ⓑ scared.

Ⓒ pushed and shoved.

Ⓓ shocked and surprised.

17. After her **retirement** from banking, Ms. Wong decided to write mystery books. What did Ms. Wong do before she wrote mystery books?

Ⓐ She wrote children's books.

Ⓑ She traveled.

Ⓒ She worked in banking.

Ⓓ She did not work.

18. A person with a lot of **patience** is likely to

Ⓐ stand in a line for two hours to ride a roller coaster.

Ⓑ complain if his pizza is not delivered within a half hour.

Ⓒ be rude to others.

Ⓓ jump ahead in a long line.

19. Which is most likely to be a **distraction** for someone who is studying?

Ⓐ good lighting

Ⓑ a noisy TV

Ⓒ an empty house

Ⓓ notes taken in class

20. You will be most likely to see a **pedestrian**

Ⓐ on a bus.

Ⓑ in a children's hospital.

Ⓒ on a horse.

Ⓓ on a sidewalk.

21. Mr. Muñez **retires** at 10:00 P.M. every night. He

Ⓐ reads at 10 P.M. every night.

Ⓑ watches the news at 10 P.M. every night.

Ⓒ goes to bed at 10 P.M. every night.

Ⓓ talks on the telephone at 10 P.M. every night.

22. Which of the following gives an **alert** that there may be a fire?

Ⓐ a smoke detector

Ⓑ a fire hose

Ⓒ an escape ladder

Ⓓ a fire extinguisher

23. What would probably happen if there were an **obstacle** in the road?

Ⓐ Traffic would speed up.

Ⓑ Traffic would slow down or stop.

Ⓒ People would carpool to work.

Ⓓ People would not know where to go.

24. Professor Mateo has **assigned** the next chapter in this book. That means that she

Ⓐ told her class to read it.
Ⓑ wrote it.
Ⓒ discussed it with her class.
Ⓓ enjoyed reading it herself.

25. A person needs be **patient** in order to

Ⓐ eat dinner.
Ⓑ wait for a delayed train.
Ⓒ play in a band.
Ⓓ go into a hospital.

26. Cats are **accustomed** to taking long naps. This means that cats

Ⓐ are made restless by taking long naps.
Ⓑ can be trained to take long naps.
Ⓒ are used to taking long naps.
Ⓓ do not like taking long naps.

27. What might happen if a passenger **distracts** the driver of a car?

Ⓐ The trip will be more fun.
Ⓑ The passenger will have to drive.
Ⓒ They are less likely to get lost.
Ⓓ An accident might occur.

Name ______________________ Date ____________

Lesson 2 Test

Find a SYNONYM for each bold word. Then fill in the circle next to your answer.

1. Purple is a **combination** of blue and red.
   - Ⓐ opposite
   - Ⓑ example
   - Ⓒ mix
   - Ⓓ result

2. Was he able to **purchase** the tickets?
   - Ⓐ locate
   - Ⓑ buy
   - Ⓒ provide
   - Ⓓ sell

3. We tried to make fresh salsa, but it tasted **bland.**
   - Ⓐ smooth
   - Ⓑ salty
   - Ⓒ delicious
   - Ⓓ flavorless

4. The **aroma** of rosemary filled the garden.
   - Ⓐ beauty
   - Ⓑ brightness
   - Ⓒ smell
   - Ⓓ quality

5. The fire **consumed** three blocks of the downtown area.
   - Ⓐ skipped
   - Ⓑ destroyed
   - Ⓒ scorched
   - Ⓓ wilted

6. That **cluster** of stars is called Orion's Belt.
   - Ⓐ group
   - Ⓑ line
   - Ⓒ pattern
   - Ⓓ glitter

7. One metric ton and 2,204 pounds are **equivalent** measures.
   - Ⓐ different
   - Ⓑ equal
   - Ⓒ large
   - Ⓓ small

8. There are cold **beverages** in the refrigerator.
   - Ⓐ desserts
   - Ⓑ drinks
   - Ⓒ snacks
   - Ⓓ salads

9. Amanda **craves** new experiences.

Ⓐ desires
Ⓑ fears
Ⓒ encounters
Ⓓ ignores

10. Mr. Yamamoto **cultivates** potatoes.

Ⓐ dislikes
Ⓑ prepares
Ⓒ sells
Ⓓ grows

Choose the best way to complete each sentence or answer each question. Then fill in the circle next to your answer.

11. To **introduce** two people, you must

Ⓐ want to get to know them.
Ⓑ know their names.
Ⓒ be sure they are friends.
Ⓓ pretend not to see them.

12. Calcium helps prevent **brittle** bones. **Brittle** bones

Ⓐ improve your posture.
Ⓑ are unusually strong.
Ⓒ break easily.
Ⓓ make you appear taller.

13. What is the best way to **extract** a splinter?

Ⓐ Use tweezers to pull it out.
Ⓑ Flatten it with a small hammer.
Ⓒ Sand it with sandpaper.
Ⓓ Put an ice cube on it.

14. After the principal's **introduction,** Mr. Sills stood up and gave his speech. Which best describes what the principal did?

Ⓐ He gave a long speech.
Ⓑ He embarrassed himself.
Ⓒ He presented a slide show.
Ⓓ He told the audience who Mr. Sills was.

15. We were surprised by the **tropical** air in the greenhouse. In this sentence, **tropical** means

Ⓐ sweet-smelling.
Ⓑ hot and dry.
Ⓒ hot and moist.
Ⓓ cold and damp.

16. Which of the following does a car **consume?**

Ⓐ gears and wheels
Ⓑ passengers
Ⓒ repair work
Ⓓ gasoline

17. To **cultivate** a child's interest in dance is to

Ⓐ discourage it.
Ⓑ encourage it.
Ⓒ not pay any attention to it.
Ⓓ make fun of it.

18. Vikram **introduced** his guests to traditional Indian foods. This means that

Ⓐ Vikram had his guests meet the cook in an Indian restaurant.
Ⓑ Vikram asked his guests to cook Indian food.
Ⓒ Vikram's guests ate Indian food for the first time.
Ⓓ Vikram's guests already enjoyed eating Indian food.

19. An **extract** from a book is

Ⓐ a review of the book.
Ⓑ a part that has been taken out of a book.
Ⓒ a summary of a book.
Ⓓ the illustrations in a book.

20. Canada **exports** lumber. This means that lumber is

Ⓐ prepared in Canada and shipped to other countries.
Ⓑ prepared in other countries and shipped in Canada.
Ⓒ is highly taxed in Canada.
Ⓓ hard to find in China.

21. America obtained valuable territory from France through the Louisiana **Purchase** in 1803. This means that America

Ⓐ lost the territory during a war with France.
Ⓑ sold the territory to France.
Ⓒ bought the territory from France.
Ⓓ traded the territory for a piece of land in France.

22. The **introduction** to a book can be found

Ⓐ in the front of the book.
Ⓑ on the back cover of the book.
Ⓒ in the back pages of the book.
Ⓓ in a magazine or newspaper.

23. Kareem was able to **extract** some information from his brother about the surprise party. What does **extract** mean in this sentence?

Ⓐ promise to someone
Ⓑ plan ahead of time
Ⓒ spread secretly
Ⓓ obtain with difficulty

24. Mr. Martin made **bland** conversation with the woman sitting next to him on the plane. Their conversation was probably

Ⓐ lively.
Ⓑ upsetting.
Ⓒ unexciting.
Ⓓ in a foreign language.

25. Which of the following is a **tropical** place?

Ⓐ the Amazon rainforest
Ⓑ the South Pole
Ⓒ the Pacific Ocean
Ⓓ New York City

26. Which of the following is the **equivalent** of 25 cents?

Ⓐ a dollar
Ⓑ a quarter
Ⓒ a dime
Ⓓ a nickel

27. Tae kwon do usually **consumes** Amy's weekends. This means that on the weekends Amy

Ⓐ has time for nothing else but tae kwon do.
Ⓑ has no time for tae kwon do.
Ⓒ often skips her tae kwon do lesson.
Ⓓ practices tae kwon do at dinnertime.

28. Rico had a **craving** for a tomato and cheese sandwich. In this sentence, **craving** means

Ⓐ a lunchbox.
Ⓑ a recipe.
Ⓒ a strong desire.
Ⓓ a strong dislike.

29. If you are unhappy with a **purchase** you made, what might you be able to do?

Ⓐ Ask the person who gave it to you to take it back.
Ⓑ Practice harder so that you will do better next time.
Ⓒ Take it back to the store and exchange it for something else.
Ⓓ Ask whether you can choose another subject.

30. Computers were **introduced** to people's homes in the early 1980s. This means that home computers

Ⓐ were invented at that time.
Ⓑ came into common use at that time.
Ⓒ were first thought of at that time.
Ⓓ were experimented with at that time.

31. The player's fans **clustered** around her. This means that the fans

Ⓐ were making a lot of noise.
Ⓑ gathered near her.
Ⓒ were shoving against her.
Ⓓ were running in circles.

32. The chef **combined** the chocolate, raspberries, and cookie crumbs. What did the chef do with these ingredients?

Ⓐ She ate them.
Ⓑ She spilled them.
Ⓒ She mixed them.
Ⓓ She chopped them.

33. To **cultivate** the land for his flower garden, Mr. Renski should

Ⓐ put up a fence.
Ⓑ plant seeds.
Ⓒ turn and fertilize the soil.
Ⓓ draw a diagram.

34. Cotton was one of America's major **exports** in the 1800s. This means that cotton was

Ⓐ a foreign product that was shipped to America.
Ⓑ a product that was needed by many American factories.
Ⓒ an American product that was shipped to other countries.
Ⓓ a raw material that was especially rare and valuable in America.

Name ______________________________ Date ______________

Test

Find an ANTONYM for each bold word. Then fill in the circle next to your answer.

1. "You may be surprised to learn that many of the large dinosaurs were not **carnivores,**" said Professor Huang.

   Ⓐ plant-eaters
   Ⓑ mammals
   Ⓒ giants
   Ⓓ swimmers

2. That little dog has a **ferocious** bark!

   Ⓐ noisy
   Ⓑ fierce
   Ⓒ mild-mannered
   Ⓓ amusing

3. The statue they are building downtown will be **gigantic** when it is finished.

   Ⓐ enormous
   Ⓑ tiny
   Ⓒ bland
   Ⓓ crude

4. Some of Ms. Frankenthaler's paintings are very **obscure.**

   Ⓐ playful
   Ⓑ exciting
   Ⓒ clear
   Ⓓ important

5. Their decision to move to Barcelona was **premature.**

   Ⓐ wise
   Ⓑ childish
   Ⓒ sound
   Ⓓ late

6. The government's aim is to **preserve** the Great Barrier Reef.

   Ⓐ fence
   Ⓑ destroy
   Ⓒ protect
   Ⓓ forget

7. The last kitten in the litter was **puny** but playful.

   Ⓐ large
   Ⓑ quiet
   Ⓒ ugly
   Ⓓ cranky

8. Field mice are the **prey** of owls and other large birds.

   Ⓐ followers
   Ⓑ relatives
   Ⓒ hunters
   Ⓓ pests

9. The extra credit assignment was **optional,** but Malik chose to do it anyway.

   Ⓐ required
   Ⓑ exciting
   Ⓒ simple
   Ⓓ difficult

10. Visitors to Hawaii can tour **extinct** volcanoes.

   Ⓐ uninteresting
   Ⓑ dangerous
   Ⓒ unattractive
   Ⓓ live

Choose the best way to complete each sentence or answer each question. Then fill in the circle next to your answer.

11. Which of the following is one of Mr. O'Brien's **ancestors?**

   Ⓐ his sister
   Ⓑ his cousin
   Ⓒ his great-grandmother
   Ⓓ his great-grandson

12. To **comprehend** a poem is to

   Ⓐ write it.
   Ⓑ understand it.
   Ⓒ discuss it thoroughly.
   Ⓓ recite it.

13. A few were injured, but every passenger **survived** the accident. This means that

   Ⓐ everyone was surprised by the accident.
   Ⓑ no one was killed.
   Ⓒ many people were at fault.
   Ⓓ everyone was seriously hurt.

14. The man in front of me in the movie theater **obscured** the screen. This means that the man

   Ⓐ made it difficult for me to see the movie.
   Ⓑ ran the theater's projector.
   Ⓒ sat in the very first row.
   Ⓓ complained that the movie was out of focus.

15. George and I salsa danced for the **duration** of the party. This means that we

   Ⓐ gave dancing lessons to the guests at the party.
   Ⓑ performed for the guests at the party.
   Ⓒ danced only at the beginning of the party.
   Ⓓ danced from the beginning to the end of the party.

16. Dodo birds and woolly mammoths are **extinct.** This means that these animals

Ⓐ are amusing to look at.
Ⓑ are hard to find.
Ⓒ no longer exist.
Ⓓ are related to one another.

17. The main purpose of a **comprehension** exam is to test

Ⓐ your ability to write.
Ⓑ your ability to multiply and divide.
Ⓒ your ability to understand something.
Ⓓ your ability to speak another language.

18. It is unfair for advertisers of car alarm systems to **prey** upon people's fears. It is unfair of advertisers to

Ⓐ break into people's cars.
Ⓑ trick people into buying car alarms systems.
Ⓒ talk people into entering the advertising business.
Ⓓ give car alarm systems away for free.

19. In the fog, the road signs were **obscure.** This means that the signs were

Ⓐ hard to read.
Ⓑ too bright.
Ⓒ wet and slippery.
Ⓓ too far apart.

20. What is someone most likely to think about the **survivor** of a plane crash?

Ⓐ He is a great pilot.
Ⓑ His family must miss him.
Ⓒ He is lucky to be alive.
Ⓓ His book is very interesting.

21. One way to **preserve** strawberries is to

Ⓐ eat them.
Ⓑ make them into jam.
Ⓒ throw them away.
Ⓓ pick them yourself.

22. My sugar cookies seemed like a **puny** contribution to the bake sale, but they helped earn over fifteen dollars. What does **puny** mean in this sentence?

Ⓐ moist and delicious
Ⓑ very generous
Ⓒ very small
Ⓓ completely tasteless

23. It is easy to become **prey** to dishonest people on the Internet. In this sentence, **prey** means

Ⓐ useful.
Ⓑ useless.
Ⓒ angry.
Ⓓ victim.

24. Which of the following would a **carnivorous** animal prefer to eat?

    Ⓐ grass
    Ⓑ leaves and branches
    Ⓒ wild fruit
    Ⓓ meat

25. The field guide said, "Today's turtles are actually very similar to their **ancestors.**" What did she mean?

    Ⓐ Turtles are like other creatures that live both on land and in the water.
    Ⓑ Turtles are like other animals that share their environment.
    Ⓒ Turtles have not changed much in a very long time.
    Ⓓ Turtles blend into the features of their environment.

26. To be given an **option** is to be

    Ⓐ told to do a certain thing.
    Ⓑ allowed to make a choice.
    Ⓒ given a punishment.
    Ⓓ told what someone else thinks or feels.

27. Birds **prey** upon insects and spiders. This means that birds

    Ⓐ hunt and eat insects and spiders.
    Ⓑ depend on insects and spiders for help.
    Ⓒ use insects and spiders in many ways.
    Ⓓ protect insects and spiders.

28. Tomás hoped that his rosebushes would **survive** the harsh winter. He wanted his rosebushes to

    Ⓐ get smaller throughout the winter.
    Ⓑ lose their thorns throughout the winter.
    Ⓒ remain alive throughout the winter.
    Ⓓ attract bees throughout the winter.

29. No one in town was quite prepared for the **ferocity** of the tornado. Which of the following is probably true about the tornado?

    Ⓐ It passed very quickly.
    Ⓑ It did not affect the town.
    Ⓒ It created a lot of damage.
    Ⓓ It was predicted far in advance.

30. Though no one believed him, it was **evident** to Galileo that Earth was round. What does **evident** mean in this sentence?

    Ⓐ hard to prove
    Ⓑ likely to be untrue
    Ⓒ humorous
    Ⓓ obvious

Name ______________________________ Date ______________

Lesson 4 Test

Find a SYNONYM for each bold word. Then fill in the circle next to your answer.

1. What can be used to **sever** the cords on a package?

Ⓐ untie
Ⓑ tie
Ⓒ cut
Ⓓ rewrap

2. The ski jumper was **jubilant** when he saw his score.

Ⓐ discouraged
Ⓑ thrilled
Ⓒ angry
Ⓓ nervous

3. Is this scale **accurate?**

Ⓐ correct
Ⓑ broken
Ⓒ fast
Ⓓ slow

4. The cruise ship will **depart** within the hour.

Ⓐ arrive
Ⓑ leave
Ⓒ sink
Ⓓ board

5. When he stopped attending study group sessions, his grades **deteriorated.**

Ⓐ worsened
Ⓑ remained
Ⓒ improved
Ⓓ recovered

6. The city needs a new bicycle **course.**

Ⓐ shop
Ⓑ rack
Ⓒ rider
Ⓓ path

7. The weather channel informed us to expect a heavy **gale** during the night.

Ⓐ snow
Ⓑ rain
Ⓒ wind
Ⓓ hail

8. The Barrys **voyaged** from Hawaii to San Francisco.

Ⓐ sailed
Ⓑ flew
Ⓒ hiked
Ⓓ chatted

Find an ANTONYM for each bold word. Then fill in the circle next to your answer.

9. A look of **despair** crossed her face when we did not find the lost dog.
   Ⓐ worry
   Ⓑ hopefulness
   Ⓒ confusion
   Ⓓ amusement

10. The Van Pragues planned their **departure** for Tuesday.
    Ⓐ party
    Ⓑ appointment
    Ⓒ flight
    Ⓓ arrival

11. A brisk walk **revived** Patrice.
    Ⓐ entertained
    Ⓑ excited
    Ⓒ tired
    Ⓓ bored

12. The music expressed everyone's **jubilation.**
    Ⓐ contentment
    Ⓑ confusion
    Ⓒ sorrow
    Ⓓ delight

13. The alligator's **approximate** weight is 150 pounds.
    Ⓐ highest
    Ⓑ exact
    Ⓒ estimated
    Ⓓ lowest

Choose the best way to complete each sentence or answer each question. Then fill in the circle next to your answer.

14. Ilyse **navigated** her raft down the Zambezi River. What does **navigated** mean in this sentence?
    Ⓐ directed
    Ⓑ lost
    Ⓒ deflated
    Ⓓ carried

15. The moon sat just above the **horizon.** The moon
    Ⓐ rose from behind a cloud.
    Ⓑ sat low in the sky.
    Ⓒ was full.
    Ⓓ was difficult to see.

16. My father becomes **nostalgic** when he

Ⓐ tries a new recipe.
Ⓑ works late at the office.
Ⓒ looks at old photographs with his sister.
Ⓓ plays basketball at the gym.

17. What is the best **course** to take if you have a bad cold? What does **course** mean in this sentence?

Ⓐ a type of medicine
Ⓑ a subject at school
Ⓒ a vacation
Ⓓ a way of acting

18. A map is **accurate** if it is

Ⓐ large.
Ⓑ correct.
Ⓒ colorful.
Ⓓ new.

19. To get ready for a **voyage,** you would be most likely to

Ⓐ order a cake.
Ⓑ paint the house.
Ⓒ pack a suitcase.
Ⓓ study hard.

20. When Mr. Russo moved, he hated to **sever** his relationships with his neighbors. In this sentence, what does **sever** mean?

Ⓐ break
Ⓑ strain
Ⓒ begin again
Ⓓ talk about

21. Which of the following is a **horizontal** line?

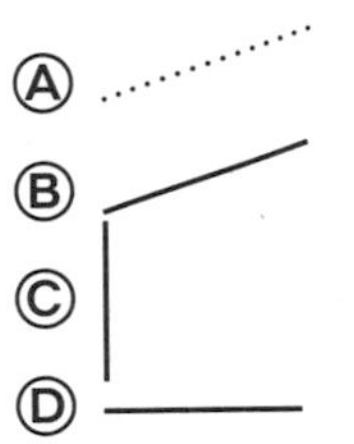

22. The Institute of **Navigation** publishes journals, hosts conferences, and grants awards. Who might be interested in joining this organization?

Ⓐ sailors and pilots
Ⓑ scientists and inventors
Ⓒ teachers and principals
Ⓓ doctors and nurses

23. When you are at your **destination,** you are

Ⓐ at the beginning of your journey.
Ⓑ in the middle of your journey.
Ⓒ at the end of your journey.
Ⓓ in a place you have never been.

24. Movies can create feelings of **nostalgia** if they are

Ⓐ set in unfamiliar countries.
Ⓑ about events that are strange and confusing.
Ⓒ full of excitement and suspense.
Ⓓ about past events that people remember fondly.

25. Which situation is most likely to make someone **despair?**

Ⓐ losing one's house in a flood
Ⓑ doing yard work
Ⓒ getting a slight sunburn
Ⓓ waiting for a bus

26. **Gales** of laughter are

Ⓐ unkind.
Ⓑ strong and noisy.
Ⓒ low and quiet.
Ⓓ short and shrill.

27. Which of the following was probably drawn with the greatest **accuracy?**

Ⓐ a sketch of a fountain
Ⓑ a cartoon of a famous person
Ⓒ a textbook diagram of a fish
Ⓓ a storybook character

28. Jonathan is working on a final paper for his zoology **course.** Which word means about the same as **course?**

Ⓐ teacher
Ⓑ project
Ⓒ partner
Ⓓ class

29. To **revive** a fashion style is to

Ⓐ invent a new style.
Ⓑ make fun of a silly style.
Ⓒ bring back a style that was in fashion at an earlier time.
Ⓓ predict which styles will be in fashion in the future.

Name ______________________ Date ______________

Lesson 5 Test

Find an ANTONYM for each bold word. Then fill in the circle next to your answer.

1. The architect used many **vertical** lines in her design.
   Ⓐ straight
   Ⓑ squiggly
   Ⓒ horizontal
   Ⓓ few

2. A famous author once said that **optimism** is the "belief that everything is beautiful, including what is ugly."
   Ⓐ hope
   Ⓑ despair
   Ⓒ intelligence
   Ⓓ stupidity

3. The chess match lasted five hours, but he finally **conquered** his opponent.
   Ⓐ challenged
   Ⓑ praised
   Ⓒ divided
   Ⓓ surrendered

4. Marta **challenged** her father's decision.
   Ⓐ forgot
   Ⓑ defended
   Ⓒ altered
   Ⓓ argued

5. His actions were **foolhardy.**
   Ⓐ weak
   Ⓑ silly
   Ⓒ wise
   Ⓓ honest

6. We made a **makeshift** fishing pole out of a yardstick and string.
   Ⓐ broken
   Ⓑ ugly
   Ⓒ large
   Ⓓ permanent

7. We had met them on a **previous** occasion.
   Ⓐ ordinary
   Ⓑ later
   Ⓒ happy
   Ⓓ rare

8. The mayor **thwarted** their efforts to build a skateboard park.
   Ⓐ blocked
   Ⓑ criticized
   Ⓒ aided
   Ⓓ praised

9. The hiker rested on the **summit** of the mountain.

   Ⓐ bottom
   Ⓑ ledge
   Ⓒ trail
   Ⓓ back

Choose the best way to complete each sentence or answer each question. Then fill in the circle next to your answer.

10. Flowers grew out of a **crevice** in the rock. What is another word for **crevice** in this sentence?

    Ⓐ canyon
    Ⓑ waterfall
    Ⓒ crack
    Ⓓ brook

11. Kai was given a new newspaper **route.** This means that she

    Ⓐ got a new bicycle to ride on.
    Ⓑ began writing articles for the newspaper.
    Ⓒ had to deliver a different newspaper.
    Ⓓ delivered papers to a different area.

12. Amber tied a **lure** to her line. **Lures** are artificial

    Ⓐ colors.
    Ⓑ fish.
    Ⓒ bait.
    Ⓓ flowers.

13. What happens during a **blizzard?**

    Ⓐ Buildings and bridges collapse.
    Ⓑ Strong winds blow and snow falls heavily.
    Ⓒ Dust covers everything.
    Ⓓ Rivers rise and flood a town.

14. An **avalanche** of mail poured into the radio station. This means that

    Ⓐ the station received a great number of letters.
    Ⓑ the station received only letters of complaint.
    Ⓒ the station received small batches of letters.
    Ⓓ letters poured in through the station's windows.

15. The hare **challenged** the tortoise to a race. The hare
    Ⓐ invited the tortoise to watch a race with him.
    Ⓑ invited the tortoise to race against him.
    Ⓒ carried the tortoise to the race grounds.
    Ⓓ did not want to race the tortoise.

16. The Spanish **conquest** of Mexico refers to
    Ⓐ when the Spanish discovered Mexico.
    Ⓑ when the Spanish explored Mexico.
    Ⓒ when the Spanish defeated and took over Mexico.
    Ⓓ when the Spanish desired to claim Mexico.

17. The family's cabin was a **makeshift** because
    Ⓐ lumber had arrived from the East.
    Ⓑ they were skilled carpenters.
    Ⓒ they planned to build a permanent cabin later.
    Ⓓ there were too many people living in it.

18. An **optimist** believes that
    Ⓐ whatever happens is a matter of luck.
    Ⓑ what's good for business is good for everyone.
    Ⓒ you should have your eyes examined regularly.
    Ⓓ good things are likely to happen.

19. The **summit** was attended by
    Ⓐ a group of swimmers.
    Ⓑ the leaders of several Asian countries.
    Ⓒ representatives from six high schools.
    Ⓓ sixty students.

20. A **terse** remark is
    Ⓐ short.
    Ⓑ funny.
    Ⓒ rude.
    Ⓓ important.

21. Which of the following could be a **challenge?**
    Ⓐ a glass of ice water
    Ⓑ a button-down shirt
    Ⓒ a postage stamp
    Ⓓ a crossword puzzle

22. We could not resist the **lure** of free concert tickets. The free tickets were
    Ⓐ phony.
    Ⓑ for terrible seats.
    Ⓒ not really free.
    Ⓓ tempting.

23. To **conquer** a bad habit is to
    Ⓐ overcome it.
    Ⓑ hate it.
    Ⓒ repeat it.
    Ⓓ develop it.

24. Something that **challenges** you

Ⓐ makes you tired.
Ⓑ requires effort.
Ⓒ makes you irritated.
Ⓓ requires a lot of money.

25. Will was **optimistic** about the weather. He said,

Ⓐ "I think it will be a beautiful day."
Ⓑ "We're going to have a nasty blizzard."
Ⓒ "The rain might spoil our picnic."
Ⓓ "I haven't heard the weather report yet."

26. I don't always take the same **route** to the beach. Sometimes I

Ⓐ wear a different swimsuit.
Ⓑ take the bus.
Ⓒ take a different path.
Ⓓ go with a different group of friends.

27. The store manager hopes the clearance sale will **lure** shoppers. The manager wants shoppers to

Ⓐ pay more for what they buy.
Ⓑ stay away from the store.
Ⓒ save money.
Ⓓ come to the store.

28. Which of the following regions is most likely to experience an **avalanche?**

Ⓐ The Gobi Desert
Ⓑ The Rocky Mountains
Ⓒ Lake Victoria
Ⓓ The Mississippi River Basin

29. Ryan was invited to participate in the diving competition, and he accepted the **challenge.** What did Ryan do?

Ⓐ He entered the competition.
Ⓑ He won first prize in the competition.
Ⓒ He decided to wait until next year's competition.
Ⓓ He was a judge for the competition.

Name ______________________________ Date ______________

Lesson 6 Test

Find a SYNONYM for each bold word. Then fill in the circle next to your answer.

1. The alarm **roused** Mr. Ramirez at 6:00 A.M.
   - Ⓐ woke
   - Ⓑ entertained
   - Ⓒ annoyed
   - Ⓓ surprised

2. "Don't **meddle** in other people's business," my grandmother said.
   - Ⓐ help
   - Ⓑ investigate
   - Ⓒ listen
   - Ⓓ interfere

3. The dog gave a yelp of **agony.**
   - Ⓐ welcome
   - Ⓑ delight
   - Ⓒ pain
   - Ⓓ fear

4. We braced ourselves for the **grim** news.
   - Ⓐ joyous
   - Ⓑ disturbing
   - Ⓒ foolhardy
   - Ⓓ interesting

5. The **steadfast** soldier stayed on watch through the night.
   - Ⓐ sleepy
   - Ⓑ loyal
   - Ⓒ hungry
   - Ⓓ patient

6. I used to **loathe** lima beans.
   - Ⓐ love
   - Ⓑ cultivate
   - Ⓒ hate
   - Ⓓ preserve

7. The Underground Railroad helped **harbor** slaves escaping from the south.
   - Ⓐ shelter
   - Ⓑ pursue
   - Ⓒ capture
   - Ⓓ return

8. The pony seemed **monstrous** next to the child.
   - Ⓐ evil
   - Ⓑ unreal
   - Ⓒ ugly
   - Ⓓ huge

9. College costs are **escalating.**

Ⓐ dropping
Ⓑ rising
Ⓒ low
Ⓓ shocking

10. We learned the Chinese **character** for "man."

Ⓐ person
Ⓑ actor
Ⓒ word
Ⓓ symbol

Choose the best way to complete each sentence or answer each question. Then fill in the circle next to your answer.

11. Cities with **harbors** are located

Ⓐ along the coast.
Ⓑ near the capital.
Ⓒ near major industrial centers.
Ⓓ near foothills.

12. A **monstrous** idea will probably cause

Ⓐ excitement.
Ⓑ applause.
Ⓒ shock.
Ⓓ concern.

13. Who might wear a **grim** expression?

Ⓐ a sales clerk making a sale
Ⓑ a child watching a clown
Ⓒ a person who has walked into a surprise party
Ⓓ a parent discussing a poor report card

14. When is someone most likely to **denounce** a friend?

Ⓐ when the friend has just walked into the room
Ⓑ when the friend disagrees about something
Ⓒ when the friend has secretly played a mean trick
Ⓓ when the friend wins an award

15. The dancer was **catapulted** into fame. This means that she

Ⓐ became famous almost overnight.
Ⓑ gradually became famous.
Ⓒ became famous against her will.
Ⓓ was soon forgotten.

16. Which of the following can illustrate someone's **character?**

Ⓐ preferring oranges to apples
Ⓑ making shy people feel welcome
Ⓒ having a portrait painted
Ⓓ getting a new haircut

17. Changes in the environment can sometimes **inflict** widespread suffering. What does **inflict** mean in this sentence?

Ⓐ relieve
Ⓑ explain
Ⓒ cause
Ⓓ avoid

18. A **meddlesome** person is most likely to

Ⓐ come up with interesting ideas.
Ⓑ make other people feel gloomy.
Ⓒ do things that shock others.
Ⓓ involve himself in someone else's affairs.

19. Because of her **loathing** of pollution, Pia started an environmental club at school. We can tell that

Ⓐ Pia does not care very much about the environment.
Ⓑ Pia hates when people pollute.
Ⓒ Pia often contributes to pollution.
Ⓓ Pia does not believe that there is anything we can do about pollution.

20. What might someone wish to **abolish?**

Ⓐ community service
Ⓑ a beautiful silver vase
Ⓒ drunken driving
Ⓓ foreign countries

21. Which of the following is most like a **catapult?**

Ⓐ a baseball
Ⓑ a football helmet
Ⓒ a slingshot
Ⓓ a broomstick

22. What are some voters most likely to **denounce?**

Ⓐ the opening of a new library
Ⓑ a campaign to keep the streets free of litter
Ⓒ a public service award to a local organization
Ⓓ a plan to raise local sales taxes

23. Which of the following might someone secretly **harbor?**

Ⓐ a strong desire to travel
Ⓑ a marble collection
Ⓒ an ear infection
Ⓓ a birthday cake

24. A story **character** is

Ⓐ a person in the story.
Ⓑ the events that take place in the story.
Ⓒ a review of a story.
Ⓓ where the story takes place.

25. The wait for the jury's decision was **agonizing.** The wait was
    Ⓐ extremely short.
    Ⓑ rather pleasant.
    Ⓒ very painful.
    Ⓓ uneventful.

26. The fourteenth through sixteenth centuries were **grim** years for Western Europe. During this time there were
    Ⓐ many new discoveries.
    Ⓑ no significant occurrences.
    Ⓒ increases in the population rate.
    Ⓓ cruel and unpleasant events.

27. The performer **roused** the unhappy crowd, so they
    Ⓐ continued to feel sad.
    Ⓑ felt excited.
    Ⓒ threw tomatoes at him.
    Ⓓ had to go home.

28. Someone who **translates** Swahili poems
    Ⓐ only reads poems written in Swahili.
    Ⓑ teaches Swahili poems in school.
    Ⓒ rewrites Swahili poems in another language.
    Ⓓ does not enjoy poetry.

Name ______________________ Date ______________

Lesson 7 Test

Find an ANTONYM for each bold word. Then fill in the circle next to your answer.

1. David gave Helena a **frigid** nod.
   Ⓐ slow
   Ⓑ gloomy
   Ⓒ cruel
   Ⓓ friendly

2. Before she became an astronaut, Sally Ride was **fascinated** by astronomy.
   Ⓐ attracted
   Ⓑ bored
   Ⓒ confused
   Ⓓ surprised

3. Jain gave us a **feeble** excuse for being late.
   Ⓐ short
   Ⓑ unclear
   Ⓒ terse
   Ⓓ believable

4. **Deposit** the money in your savings account.
   Ⓐ remove
   Ⓑ put
   Ⓒ ignore
   Ⓓ count

5. There's a **remote** chance that he'll win the race.
   Ⓐ slim
   Ⓑ possible
   Ⓒ upsetting
   Ⓓ great

6. That sofa bed is a **substantial** piece of furniture.
   Ⓐ heavy
   Ⓑ small
   Ⓒ useful
   Ⓓ ugly

7. The team was shocked by the coach's **harsh** words.
   Ⓐ kind
   Ⓑ ordinary
   Ⓒ expected
   Ⓓ discouraging

Choose the best way to complete each sentence or answer each question. Then fill in the circle next to your answer.

8. Rashid needs to wear **formal** attire to his brother's party. What should he wear?

   Ⓐ a suit and tie
   Ⓑ a bathing suit
   Ⓒ a t-shirt and shorts
   Ⓓ his pajamas

9. A **substantial** loss is a

   Ⓐ sudden loss.
   Ⓑ great loss.
   Ⓒ small loss.
   Ⓓ discouraging loss.

10. Which of the following walks with a **waddle?**

    Ⓐ a crow
    Ⓑ a runner
    Ⓒ a duck
    Ⓓ a dancer

11. The rugby team **deposited** their equipment in the locker room. What does **deposited** mean in this sentence?

    Ⓐ locked up
    Ⓑ used
    Ⓒ repaired
    Ⓓ laid down

12. A **colony** of mushrooms is growing on the lawn. The mushrooms are

    Ⓐ scattered all over.
    Ⓑ clustered together.
    Ⓒ all the same size and shape.
    Ⓓ going to be there for a short while.

13. The workers will be **compensated** for working overtime. They will be

    Ⓐ told to work more quickly.
    Ⓑ lectured by the boss.
    Ⓒ paid extra money.
    Ⓓ questioned about their work habits.

14. Which of the following is most likely to have a **remote** control?

    Ⓐ a shower
    Ⓑ an oven
    Ⓒ a television
    Ⓓ a microscope

15. The class president has very **rigid** ideas. This means that

    Ⓐ she likes to share her ideas with others.
    Ⓑ she is very intelligent.
    Ⓒ she comes up with unusual solutions to problems.
    Ⓓ nothing will change her way of thinking.

16. You might **huddle** on the floor of your closet if you are
    - Ⓐ trying to hide.
    - Ⓑ looking for a shoe.
    - Ⓒ cleaning your closet.
    - Ⓓ throwing things in there to hide them.

17. A **solitary** hiker is
    - Ⓐ hiking alone.
    - Ⓑ highly experienced.
    - Ⓒ leading a group.
    - Ⓓ walking very slowly.

18. There is a **deposit** of silt at the mouth of the river. What does **deposit** mean in this sentence?
    - Ⓐ something taken away
    - Ⓑ something laid down
    - Ⓒ a mountain
    - Ⓓ a brook

19. The team **huddled** on the field. They
    - Ⓐ played well.
    - Ⓑ were defeated.
    - Ⓒ practiced.
    - Ⓓ gathered together.

20. **Harsh** colors are
    - Ⓐ bright and cheerful.
    - Ⓑ unpleasant.
    - Ⓒ soft and pale.
    - Ⓓ glossy.

21. Ms. Medina's town was very **remote** and had just one dirt road running through it. What does **remote** mean in this sentence?
    - Ⓐ cold
    - Ⓑ old
    - Ⓒ far away
    - Ⓓ small

22. André lost his friend's favorite baseball card and he wants to **compensate** her. What should he do?
    - Ⓐ buy her another baseball card
    - Ⓑ buy her a soda
    - Ⓒ apologize
    - Ⓓ ask to borrow another baseball card

23. New York was once a **colony** of the Netherlands. This means that New York
    - Ⓐ once traded with the Netherlands.
    - Ⓑ once fought the Netherlands in a war.
    - Ⓒ once ruled the Netherlands.
    - Ⓓ once had legal ties to the Netherlands.

24. A person who **waddles**
    - Ⓐ is an excellent swimmer.
    - Ⓑ can never make up his mind.
    - Ⓒ sways from side to side when he walks.
    - Ⓓ makes many mistakes.

25. There was a **solitary** cloud in the sky. The cloud was
    - Ⓐ dark and threatening.
    - Ⓑ the only one in the sky.
    - Ⓒ shaped like a familiar object.
    - Ⓓ passing quickly.

26. When you make a **deposit** at the bank, you are
    - Ⓐ applying for a job.
    - Ⓑ applying for a credit card.
    - Ⓒ taking money out of your account.
    - Ⓓ putting money into your account.

27. Robyn said, "*Shackleton's Antarctic Adventure* was a **fascinating** movie." How did Robyn feel about the movie?
    - Ⓐ It was long and boring.
    - Ⓑ It was difficult to understand.
    - Ⓒ It was interesting and exciting.
    - Ⓓ It was scary and upsetting.

28. When would you be most likely to write a **formal** letter?
    - Ⓐ to complain about the service you received at a restaurant
    - Ⓑ to thank your grandparents for your birthday present
    - Ⓒ to send a postcard to your friend
    - Ⓓ to invite your cousin to your graduation party

29. If something makes you **feeble,** it makes you
    - Ⓐ laugh a long time.
    - Ⓑ think very hard about something.
    - Ⓒ feel weak.
    - Ⓓ feel sorry.

30. The sheep were in a **huddle** beside the barn. The sheep were
    - Ⓐ grazing peacefully.
    - Ⓑ crowded together.
    - Ⓒ in a line.
    - Ⓓ making a lot of noise.

31. As **compensation** for missing her basketball game, Gabby's dad took her to the park. Why did he take her to the park?
    - Ⓐ He felt sorry that he missed the game and wanted to make it up to her.
    - Ⓑ He thought that she needed to practice basketball.
    - Ⓒ He wanted to play basketball with his friends.
    - Ⓓ He does not enjoy playing basketball.

32. The settlers in North Dakota lived under **harsh** conditions. They
    - Ⓐ never had to worry about good harvests.
    - Ⓑ often had pleasant rainstorms.
    - Ⓒ had to follow the rules of the community.
    - Ⓓ had to struggle with freezing winters.

33. Owen was worried that his brother was acting **remote.** How was his brother acting?

    Ⓐ distant and isolated
    Ⓑ childish and immature
    Ⓒ forgetful and absent-minded
    Ⓓ angry and cruel

34. Rachel **resembles** her grandmother in many ways. This means that Rachel

    Ⓐ does not get along with her grandmother.
    Ⓑ is very fond of her grandmother.
    Ⓒ takes care of her grandmother.
    Ⓓ looks and acts like her grandmother.

35. Which of the following is **rigid?**

    Ⓐ ice cream
    Ⓑ a ball of twine
    Ⓒ a steel rod
    Ⓓ a bag of rice

36. What could make someone feel **frigid?**

    Ⓐ lying in the shade on a hot day
    Ⓑ waiting for the bus on a cold winter morning
    Ⓒ hearing a spooky sound in the night
    Ⓓ eating a very large meal

Name ______________________ Date ______________

Lesson 8 Test

Find a SYNONYM for each bold word. Then fill in the circle next to your answer.

1. Were you invited to attend the **banquet?**
   - Ⓐ concert
   - Ⓑ meeting
   - Ⓒ feast
   - Ⓓ performance

2. The three of them **pledged** to keep the secret forever.
   - Ⓐ agreed
   - Ⓑ promised
   - Ⓒ decided
   - Ⓓ failed

3. I was assigned a difficult **task.**
   - Ⓐ job
   - Ⓑ role
   - Ⓒ route
   - Ⓓ challenge

4. The kids' request for more games seemed **frivolous.**
   - Ⓐ reasonable
   - Ⓑ confusing
   - Ⓒ optimistic
   - Ⓓ silly

5. The boat will sail as soon as the **cargo** is aboard.
   - Ⓐ crew
   - Ⓑ passengers
   - Ⓒ fuel
   - Ⓓ load

6. The olives were **harvested** last week.
   - Ⓐ canned
   - Ⓑ sprayed
   - Ⓒ gathered
   - Ⓓ shipped

7. What time is the **assembly?**
   - Ⓐ departure
   - Ⓑ meeting
   - Ⓒ arrival
   - Ⓓ movie

8. The travelers were in a **desperate** situation.
   - Ⓐ hopeless
   - Ⓑ unusual
   - Ⓒ fortunate
   - Ⓓ unexpected

Find an ANTONYM for each bold word. Then fill in the circle next to your answer.

9. The new Lebanese restaurant is likely to **prosper.**

Ⓐ succeed
Ⓑ cater
Ⓒ fail
Ⓓ grow

10. Mr. Harris **decreased** his sons' allowances.

Ⓐ remembered
Ⓑ discussed
Ⓒ delayed
Ⓓ raised

11. The class **assembled** in the courtyard after the first bell.

Ⓐ shouted
Ⓑ ran
Ⓒ scattered
Ⓓ hurried

12. If you are ever in France, you will see that it is not true that the French are **hostile** to tourists.

Ⓐ cruel
Ⓑ welcoming
Ⓒ uninterested
Ⓓ usual

13. A **celebrated** author visited our class and talked about her books.

Ⓐ unknown
Ⓑ untalented
Ⓒ well-liked
Ⓓ nonfiction

14. Her **frivolity** made a poor impression on the principal.

Ⓐ intelligence
Ⓑ cleanliness
Ⓒ seriousness
Ⓓ promptness

Choose the best way to complete each sentence or answer each question. Then fill in the circle next to your answer.

15. Which of the following are **edibles?**

Ⓐ magazines and newspapers
Ⓑ diamonds and pearls
Ⓒ computers and typewriters
Ⓓ apples and pears

16. Which of the following can be used as a **cask?**

Ⓐ a wagon
Ⓑ a barrel
Ⓒ a small box
Ⓓ a coffin

17. What would someone use to **hew** a tree?

Ⓐ a chainsaw
Ⓑ an ax
Ⓒ a crane
Ⓓ a strong rope

18. When it's **harvest** time, farmers

Ⓐ sit down and have lunch.
Ⓑ have a feast.
Ⓒ gather crops.
Ⓓ plant seeds.

19. Margot and her father **assembled** the swing set. What did Margot and her father do to the swing set?

Ⓐ They took it apart.
Ⓑ They put it together.
Ⓒ They repaired it.
Ⓓ They built it from scratch.

20. Many people **celebrate** the Chinese New Year in late January or early February. What does **celebrate** mean in this sentence?

Ⓐ forget
Ⓑ honor
Ⓒ know about
Ⓓ do not care about

21. The **Pledge** of Allegiance is

Ⓐ a failure to be faithful.
Ⓑ a promise to be faithful.
Ⓒ beginning to be faithful.
Ⓓ stopping being faithful.

22. A **prosperous** business has

Ⓐ many products.
Ⓑ many workers.
Ⓒ much success.
Ⓓ little success.

23. If a TV show experiences a **decrease** in viewers, it means that the show is being watched

Ⓐ by fewer people.
Ⓑ by more people.
Ⓒ by younger people.
Ⓓ by older people.

24. Alisha was **desperate** to find her lost dog. How did Alisha feel?

Ⓐ satisfied
Ⓑ joyous
Ⓒ tired
Ⓓ despairing

25. An **edible** mushroom is

Ⓐ native to the region.
Ⓑ safe to eat.
Ⓒ poisonous.
Ⓓ rare.

26. How might an audience show **hostility?**

Ⓐ by clapping loudly
Ⓑ by coughing
Ⓒ by booing
Ⓓ by falling asleep

27. A good **harvest** is

Ⓐ a well-built machine.
Ⓑ a large quantity of crops.
Ⓒ a terrific party.
Ⓓ an excellent book.

28. To **hew** a tree-trunk canoe is to

Ⓐ paddle it quickly.
Ⓑ paint decorations on it.
Ⓒ carve it with an ax.
Ⓓ push it into the water.

29. If "no **assembly** required" is written on a box, what does that mean?

Ⓐ You will not have to put the contents together.
Ⓑ You will have to put the contents together.
Ⓒ The contents do not include batteries.
Ⓓ The contents are heavy.

Name ______________________________ Date ______________

Test

Find a SYNONYM for each bold word. Then fill in the circle next to your answer.

1. My subscription will **terminate** at the end of the month.

   Ⓐ begin
   Ⓑ change
   Ⓒ end
   Ⓓ increase

2. Home prices are **soaring.**

   Ⓐ decreasing
   Ⓑ rising
   Ⓒ dropping
   Ⓓ changing

3. I have a **significant** reason for asking you here.

   Ⓐ secret
   Ⓑ personal
   Ⓒ embarrassing
   Ⓓ important

4. The **heroic** dog dragged the duckling to safety.

   Ⓐ huge
   Ⓑ weary
   Ⓒ brave
   Ⓓ strong

5. The **experiment** showed that Dr. Yuan was correct.

   Ⓐ test
   Ⓑ report
   Ⓒ article
   Ⓓ committee

6. We all saw through Nikki's **flimsy** excuse.

   Ⓐ rude
   Ⓑ feeble
   Ⓒ believable
   Ⓓ embarrassing

Find an ANTONYM for each bold word. Then fill in the circle next to your answer.

7. John came up with an **absurd** plan.
   Ⓐ detailed
   Ⓑ foolish
   Ⓒ ingenious
   Ⓓ simple

8. Uncle Ike **lumbered** into the room.
   Ⓐ stamped
   Ⓑ stomped
   Ⓒ glided
   Ⓓ waddled

9. The **spectators** left the field.
   Ⓐ crowd
   Ⓑ players
   Ⓒ fans
   Ⓓ pigeons

10. Gerard's stunt kite was **soaring.**
   Ⓐ falling
   Ⓑ sailing
   Ⓒ rising
   Ⓓ bobbing

11. Federico felt **dense** because he hadn't done his homework.
   Ⓐ interested
   Ⓑ clever
   Ⓒ bored
   Ⓓ sleepy

Choose the best way to complete each sentence or answer each question. Then fill in the circle next to your answer.

12. An **unwieldy** suitcase is
   Ⓐ unmarked.
   Ⓑ sturdy.
   Ⓒ satisfactory.
   Ⓓ hard to handle.

13. A **mimic** is someone who
   Ⓐ is shorter than usual.
   Ⓑ is involved in the government.
   Ⓒ imitates the actions of others.
   Ⓓ is under the age of 21.

14. Maya **suspended** the hammock in the back yard. What does **suspended** mean in this sentence?
   Ⓐ wove
   Ⓑ sat on
   Ⓒ broke
   Ⓓ hung

15. Which of the following is a true **accomplishment?**
    - Ⓐ taking a bath
    - Ⓑ trying out for a play
    - Ⓒ playing the piano well
    - Ⓓ going shopping

16. The rainforest was **dense.** This means that
    - Ⓐ no one lived in it.
    - Ⓑ its trees grew close together.
    - Ⓒ it was humid.
    - Ⓓ it was being destroyed.

17. To **experiment** with sound waves is to
    - Ⓐ design tests to discover more about sound waves.
    - Ⓑ play a musical instrument.
    - Ⓒ read about sound waves.
    - Ⓓ show sound waves with diagrams.

18. When you **ascend** a flight of stairs, you are
    - Ⓐ going up.
    - Ⓑ coming down.
    - Ⓒ taking an elevator.
    - Ⓓ building a flight of stairs.

19. Classes might be **suspended** because
    - Ⓐ the community voted for longer school days.
    - Ⓑ an important state official is visiting.
    - Ⓒ a heavy snowfall has closed the roads.
    - Ⓓ someone was fooling around in class.

20. At the zoo, Bernard **mimicked** the penguins. This means that he
    - Ⓐ liked the penguins best.
    - Ⓑ tried to attract the penguins.
    - Ⓒ copied the behavior of the penguins.
    - Ⓓ disliked the penguins.

21. You can **accomplish** many things if you
    - Ⓐ are forgetful.
    - Ⓑ live in a major city.
    - Ⓒ join a committee.
    - Ⓓ make a strong effort.

22. The school replaced the **flimsy** tables and chairs in the cafeteria. What does **flimsy** mean in this sentence?
    - Ⓐ poorly made
    - Ⓑ covered with fabric
    - Ⓒ pale green
    - Ⓓ sturdily built

23. What can **lumber** be used for?
    Ⓐ to season dishes
    Ⓑ to paint pictures
    Ⓒ to build houses
    Ⓓ to power lamps

24. A **dense** fog
    Ⓐ is difficult to see through.
    Ⓑ causes heavy rain.
    Ⓒ is a light fog.
    Ⓓ causes cold weather.

25. Paula was **suspended** from the girls lacrosse team. This means that
    Ⓐ she didn't make the team this year.
    Ⓑ she is off the team for now.
    Ⓒ her teammates dislike her.
    Ⓓ she got a cheer from her teammates.

26. Marco **experimented** with his hair. He
    Ⓐ went to the same barber.
    Ⓑ put a blue streak in it.
    Ⓒ shampooed it every day.
    Ⓓ complained about it to his friends.

27. The roofers made a **heroic** effort to put on the new roof during the storm. This means that the roofers
    Ⓐ were seldom on time.
    Ⓑ were fun to watch as they worked.
    Ⓒ failed to get the job done on time.
    Ⓓ worked especially hard to get the job done.

28. Brandon **mimicked** Mr. James. He was sent to the principal's office because
    Ⓐ he talked back to Mr. James.
    Ⓑ he refused to answer Mr. James.
    Ⓒ he made fun of Mr. James by imitating him.
    Ⓓ he annoyed Mr. James by fooling around.

29. Ryan didn't quite appreciate the **significance** of his graduation. His graduation was
    Ⓐ a terrible experience to get through.
    Ⓑ a tiresome activity.
    Ⓒ an important day in his life.
    Ⓓ a warning of worse things to come.

Name ______________________________ Date ______________

Test

Find a SYNONYM for each bold word. Then fill in the circle next to your answer.

1. Harold had a **yearning** for a pet.
   Ⓐ dislike
   Ⓑ longing
   Ⓒ location
   Ⓓ puppy

2. Mr. Lombardo thinks that this brand of peanut butter is **superior.**
   Ⓐ fine
   Ⓑ chunky
   Ⓒ worst
   Ⓓ best

3. We are **reluctant** to make the long trip.
   Ⓐ eager
   Ⓑ prepared
   Ⓒ unwilling
   Ⓓ anxious

4. Photography is one of Joab's **pursuits.**
   Ⓐ skills
   Ⓑ classes
   Ⓒ hobbies
   Ⓓ dislikes

5. Heather will **donate** a hundred dollars to the organization.
   Ⓐ give
   Ⓑ request
   Ⓒ repay
   Ⓓ lend

6. David gave his teacher an **evasive** answer.
   Ⓐ prompt
   Ⓑ careful
   Ⓒ incorrect
   Ⓓ indirect

Find an ANTONYM for each bold word. Then fill in the circle next to your answer.

7. After 27 years, Nelson Mandela was finally **liberated** from prison.

Ⓐ interviewed
Ⓑ arrested
Ⓒ hired
Ⓓ freed

8. The twins have **numerous** interests.

Ⓐ few
Ⓑ celebrated
Ⓒ usual
Ⓓ boring

9. The Emancipation Proclamation released slaves from **bondage.**

Ⓐ kindness
Ⓑ freedom
Ⓒ concern
Ⓓ home

10. Park rules **prohibit** dogs.

Ⓐ mention
Ⓑ forbid
Ⓒ allow
Ⓓ ignore

Choose the best way to complete each sentence or answer each question. Then fill in the circle next to your answer.

11. Someone who is your **superior** is

Ⓐ smarter than you are.
Ⓑ unpleasant to you.
Ⓒ someone who teases you.
Ⓓ higher in rank than you are.

12. To **pursue** an interest is to

Ⓐ give time and energy to it.
Ⓑ give it up.
Ⓒ ask questions about it.
Ⓓ talk about it often.

13. How could a cat **evade** a dog?

Ⓐ by climbing a tree
Ⓑ by hissing at the dog
Ⓒ by scratching the dog's nose
Ⓓ by becoming friends with the dog

14. Someone who **establishes** an organization is

Ⓐ a frequent visitor to the organization.
Ⓑ the person who creates the organization.
Ⓒ a worker for the organization.
Ⓓ someone who respects the organization.

15. What could be a community **occasion?**

Ⓐ litter on the streets
Ⓑ a small population
Ⓒ an Independence Day parade
Ⓓ an after-school club

16. If you were in a debate, who would the **opposition** be?

Ⓐ your teammates
Ⓑ the audience
Ⓒ the judges
Ⓓ the other debate team

17. If tickets for a play are **available,** then

Ⓐ they are very expensive.
Ⓑ they are sold out.
Ⓒ they are easy to get.
Ⓓ you can no longer buy them.

18. He **evaded** the question. What does **evaded** mean in this sentence?

Ⓐ answered
Ⓑ avoided
Ⓒ resented
Ⓓ asked

19. When you feel **reluctance** to go someplace, you

Ⓐ can't wait to go.
Ⓑ don't really want to go.
Ⓒ feel lucky to have been invited.
Ⓓ feel homesick.

20. Which of the following is a good example of an **establishment?**

Ⓐ a street sign.
Ⓑ a picnic table.
Ⓒ a restroom.
Ⓓ a hotel.

21. What is the purpose of a **pursuit?**

Ⓐ to capture someone or something
Ⓑ to check your account
Ⓒ to summarize information
Ⓓ to state a position

22. In the army, a general is **superior** to a captain. This means that

Ⓐ a captain ranks higher than a general.
Ⓑ a general ranks higher than a captain.
Ⓒ a general is equal to a captain.
Ⓓ a general is an advisor to a captain.

23. The committee **established** that errors had been made in the lab. What does **established** mean?

Ⓐ found to be true
Ⓑ charged wrongfully
Ⓒ complained
Ⓓ denied

24. You and I have spoken on several **occasions.** We have spoken

Ⓐ on several committees.
Ⓑ on several topics.
Ⓒ several times.
Ⓓ at several presidential elections.

25. An example of a **donation** is

Ⓐ a check for $50.
Ⓑ a request for funds.
Ⓒ a charity.
Ⓓ a report on finances.

26. To **yearn** is to

Ⓐ groan about something.
Ⓑ long for something.
Ⓒ plan something.
Ⓓ struggle to get something.

27. To **oppose** something is to

Ⓐ study it carefully.
Ⓑ act against it.
Ⓒ prohibit it.
Ⓓ support it.

28. What might a cat **pursue?**

Ⓐ a dog
Ⓑ cat food
Ⓒ a long nap
Ⓓ a mouse

29. To have **occasional** headaches is to have

Ⓐ painful headaches.
Ⓑ mild headaches.
Ⓒ headaches every once in a while.
Ⓓ frequent headaches.

30. If the doctor **reassures** you about your illness, you will probably

Ⓐ begin to worry about it.
Ⓑ give up hope.
Ⓒ feel less worried about it.
Ⓓ go straight to the hospital.

31. During the storm, passengers asked the flight attendant for **reassurance.** They wanted him to

Ⓐ give them their money back.
Ⓑ bring them food and beverages.
Ⓒ tell them that they would be safe.
Ⓓ update them on their likely time of arrival.

Name ____ Date ________________

Midterm Test 1

Read the passage. Choose the best answer for each sentence or question about a bold word. Then fill in the circle next to your answer.

The Early Days of Air Travel

When passenger air travel was **introduced** to Europe in the 1920s, it was at first rough and uncomfortable. The planes were noisy, unheated, and able to hold only a few people. However, flying from England to France was much quicker than crossing the English Channel by boat. A plane could **depart** from London and arrive in Paris in a mere three hours. It was no wonder the number of Europeans traveling by plane **soared** during this decade.

Airlines did all they could to make flying attractive and to convince the public that air travel was a **superior** form of transportation. They emphasized, of course, the speed of planes. They also stressed that flying was safe. They tried many things to **lure** customers. Some airlines even called attention to some **celebrated** people who calmly traveled by air.

Over the next 20 years, **substantial** changes took place in air travel. The planes became quieter and more comfortable. Meals were served on the flights. In America, the first air "hostess," a trained nurse, was hired in 1930. Traveling in an American DC3 was the height of luxury in the 1930s. DC3 airplanes carried no more than 14 passengers. Sleeping platforms folded down from a wall, and curtains provided privacy as the passengers slept. In the morning, they were **roused** by a crew member bringing breakfast foods and hot **beverages** on a tray. By 1932, the **duration** of a cross-country flight—with several stops—had been reduced to 24 hours.

Air travel has taken great steps forward since its early days. After all, our **gigantic** planes cross the continent in no more than six hours. However, some passengers who have become **accustomed** to being cramped in narrow seats for the entire afternoon cannot help but wonder if every change has been for the better.

1. Read this sentence from the passage.

   When passenger air travel was introduced to Europe in the 1920s, it was at first rough and uncomfortable.

   What does **introduced** mean in this passage?

   Ⓐ made known by name
   Ⓑ brought into use
   Ⓒ called to someone's attention
   Ⓓ welcomed as a guest speaker

2. Read this sentence from the passage.

   A plane could depart from London and arrive in Paris in a mere three hours.

   A SYNONYM for **depart** is

   Ⓐ arrive.
   Ⓑ arise.
   Ⓒ leave.
   Ⓓ escalate.

3. Read these words from the passage.

   . . . the number of Europeans traveling by plane soared during this decade . . .

   In this passage, **soared** means

   Ⓐ suddenly became greater.
   Ⓑ flew like a bird.
   Ⓒ coasted.
   Ⓓ began to descend.

4. Read these words from the passage.

   . . . air travel was a superior form of transportation.

   What is another word for **superior?**

   Ⓐ speedy
   Ⓑ useful
   Ⓒ reasonable
   Ⓓ excellent

5. Read this sentence from the passage.

   They tried many things to lure customers.

   What is a SYNONYM for **lure?**

   Ⓐ bait
   Ⓑ trick
   Ⓒ attract
   Ⓓ comfort

6. Read these words from the passage.

   Some airlines even called attention to some celebrated people . . .

   What is a SYNONYM for **celebrated?**

   Ⓐ rich
   Ⓑ famous
   Ⓒ fearless
   Ⓓ remarkable

7. Read this sentence from the passage.

   Over the next 20 years, substantial changes took place in air travel.

   What does **substantial** mean in this passage?

   Ⓐ very heavy
   Ⓑ sudden
   Ⓒ expensive
   Ⓓ many

8. Read these words from the passage.

   . . . they were roused by a crew member . . .

   What is a SYNONYM for **roused?**

   Ⓐ awakened
   Ⓑ fed
   Ⓒ excited
   Ⓓ called

9. Read these words from the passage.

   . . . bringing breakfast foods and hot* beverages *. . .

   A SYNONYM for **beverages** is

   Ⓐ towels.
   Ⓑ water.
   Ⓒ drinks.
   Ⓓ cereals.

10. Read these words from the passage.

    . . . the* duration *of a cross-country flight . . .

    In this passage, **duration** means

    Ⓐ the speed of the flight.
    Ⓑ the length of the flight.
    Ⓒ the distance of the flight.
    Ⓓ the number of people on the flight.

11. Read this sentence from the passage.

    After all, our* gigantic *planes cross the continent in no more than six hours.

    What is a SYNONYM for **gigantic?**

    Ⓐ huge
    Ⓑ noisy
    Ⓒ uncomfortable
    Ⓓ modern

12. Read these words from the passage.

    . . . some passengers who have become* accustomed *to being cramped in narrow seats . . .

    What does this mean?

    Ⓐ Some passengers are directed to narrow seats.
    Ⓑ Some passengers are hostile to narrow seats.
    Ⓒ Some passengers are assigned to narrow seats.
    Ⓓ Some passengers are used to sitting in narrow seats.

Name ______________________________ Date ______________

Midterm Test 2

Read the passage. Choose the best answer for each sentence or question about a bold word. Then fill in the circle next to your answer.

The Donner Party

Though the pioneer times were an exciting era in American history, not all pioneer tales are success stories. In 1846, a wagon train of farm families led by George Donner left Illinois. Their **destination** was California—2,000 miles away. When they arrived in Utah, members of the group talked the others into using a shortcut. The **route** was supposed to be shorter and easier for the pioneers, but the land was unfamiliar to them and they wasted valuable time trying to find their way. Their wagons reached the Sierras just as heavy winter snows were due.

When the Donner party was deep in the mountains, a severe winter storm trapped them. They made camp where they were, moving into one deserted cabin and building several **makeshift** ones. Unfortunately, the winter was unusually **harsh** and their attempts to continue on were unsuccessful.

They soon **consumed** all the food that they had **available,** and they were unable to find much game or **edible** plants in the frozen mountains. They used extreme measures to stay alive. The party ate a thick soup made from the hides of their dead cattle.

After two **grim** months in the mountains, all were starving and feeling **desperate.** Fifteen people volunteered to go on snowshoes to California and get help. Of all those in the camp, they were the strongest. Many of their **companions** had died or were very ill. Eight members of this **heroic** band died along the way. When the remaining seven reached California, it was a month before rescue teams could reach the stranded party. Of the 78 people who had been trapped in the mountains, only 45 **survived.** Twelve-year-old Virginia Reed was one of them. When asked about her experience in the mountains, she gave this advice: "Never take no cut-offs and hurry along as fast as you can."

1. According to this passage, what is a **destination?**

   Ⓐ a path to follow
   Ⓑ someone's home country
   Ⓒ someone's starting place
   Ⓓ the place to which someone is going

2. In this passage, **route** means

   Ⓐ the guide of a wagon train.
   Ⓑ the end of the wagon train.
   Ⓒ a course that one follows to get somewhere.
   Ⓓ a superhighway.

3. A **makeshift** cabin is

   Ⓐ a cabin made out of stone.
   Ⓑ a mountain home.
   Ⓒ a place for hunters to stay.
   Ⓓ a temporary place to live.

4. A **harsh** winter is likely to be

   Ⓐ milder than usual.
   Ⓑ very cold with many blizzards.
   Ⓒ longer than usual.
   Ⓓ sometimes sunny and sometimes snowy.

5. In this passage, what does **consumed** mean?

   Ⓐ destroyed
   Ⓑ spent
   Ⓒ ate
   Ⓓ cooked

6. What does **available** mean in this passage?

   Ⓐ paid for
   Ⓑ carried along
   Ⓒ used up
   Ⓓ ready to use

7. **Edible** plants

   Ⓐ can be eaten.
   Ⓑ grow in the winter.
   Ⓒ are found in mountains.
   Ⓓ are easy to spot.

8. The party was trapped for two **grim** months. You can tell that those months must have been

   Ⓐ difficult and painful.
   Ⓑ between September and February.
   Ⓒ in the middle of winter.
   Ⓓ longer than usual.

9. Which of these words is the best SYNONYM for **desperate?**

   Ⓐ angry
   Ⓑ trapped
   Ⓒ hopeless
   Ⓓ weak

10. A **companion** is

    Ⓐ someone who has to be cared for.
    Ⓑ someone you spend time with.
    Ⓒ a person whom you do not trust.
    Ⓓ a person in a dangerous situation.

11. Which is a SYNONYM for **heroic?**

Ⓐ courageous
Ⓑ foolhardy
Ⓒ famous
Ⓓ loyal

12. Only 45 people **survived.** What does **survived** mean in this passage?

Ⓐ were still able to walk
Ⓑ remained alive
Ⓒ decided to continue
Ⓓ perished

Name ______________________ Date ____________

Lesson 11 Test

Find a SYNONYM for each bold word. Then fill in the circle next to your answer.

1. New technologies **accelerated** change in the 20th century.

   Ⓐ challenged
   Ⓑ guided
   Ⓒ slowed
   Ⓓ hurried

2. She performed a **methodical** search for the missing report.

   Ⓐ nervous
   Ⓑ orderly
   Ⓒ optimistic
   Ⓓ careless

3. Kim **exulted** over her test score.

   Ⓐ rejoiced
   Ⓑ cried
   Ⓒ apologized
   Ⓓ repented

4. The sea air is **bracing.**

   Ⓐ windy
   Ⓑ smelly
   Ⓒ refreshing
   Ⓓ warm

5. Jessie is **anxious** to go on vacation.

   Ⓐ packing
   Ⓑ reluctant
   Ⓒ planning
   Ⓓ eager

6. Dr. Halloran **sauntered** down the street.

   Ⓐ darted
   Ⓑ strolled
   Ⓒ staggered
   Ⓓ waddled

7. One **stall** at the fair had bamboo plants for sale.

   Ⓐ booth
   Ⓑ person
   Ⓒ florist
   Ⓓ family

Find an ANTONYM for each bold word. Then fill in the circle next to your answer.

8. What is the **maximum** number of people that can be seated in this auditorium?
   - Ⓐ average
   - Ⓑ largest
   - Ⓒ smallest
   - Ⓓ usual

9. His **solo** skating routine received a lot of applause.
   - Ⓐ dull
   - Ⓑ dancing
   - Ⓒ clumsy
   - Ⓓ team

10. I have **confidence** in her ability to do the work.
    - Ⓐ belief
    - Ⓑ certainty
    - Ⓒ doubt
    - Ⓓ recommendations

11. We were **exultant** after the championship game.
    - Ⓐ jubilant
    - Ⓑ restless
    - Ⓒ depressed
    - Ⓓ tired

12. Quiet, everyone! It's time to **proceed.**
    - Ⓐ begin
    - Ⓑ pause
    - Ⓒ eliminate
    - Ⓓ continue

Choose the best way to complete each sentence or answer each question. Then fill in the circle next to your answer.

13. What is most likely to cause **anxiety?**
    - Ⓐ giving a speech
    - Ⓑ getting a haircut
    - Ⓒ listening to music
    - Ⓓ buying groceries

14. Justin tried to **stall** his punishment. This means that he tried to
    - Ⓐ blame someone else for what he'd done.
    - Ⓑ shorten his punishment.
    - Ⓒ put his punishment off.
    - Ⓓ get out of his punishment altogether.

15. Which of the following might need a **brace?**

    Ⓐ a sandwich
    Ⓑ a flat tire
    Ⓒ a broken lamp
    Ⓓ a sprained ankle

16. I am in **contact** with the babysitter. This means that

    Ⓐ the babysitter and I agree on most things.
    Ⓑ the babysitter and I communicate.
    Ⓒ the babysitter will be over shortly.
    Ⓓ the babysitter lives near me.

17. What could be scary about **soloing?**

    Ⓐ You might lose your music.
    Ⓑ You could lose your balance.
    Ⓒ The boat could tip over.
    Ⓓ No one else is there to help you fly the plane.

18. Jorge and Christine took a **saunter** along the trail. They

    Ⓐ walked slowly.
    Ⓑ rode their bikes.
    Ⓒ took photographs.
    Ⓓ took a guest.

19. A **nonchalant** person seems to

    Ⓐ be afraid of challenges.
    Ⓑ take nothing seriously.
    Ⓒ act rudely at times.
    Ⓓ fear the worst.

20. Which of the following is most likely to be kept in a **stall?**

    Ⓐ a car
    Ⓑ a horse
    Ⓒ bags of flour
    Ⓓ an airplane

21. What might be described in terms of its **altitude?**

    Ⓐ a racecar
    Ⓑ a difficult student
    Ⓒ a mountain
    Ⓓ a sailboat

22. He tried to **brace** himself for the bad news. In this sentence, **brace** means

    Ⓐ ask.
    Ⓑ prepare.
    Ⓒ inform.
    Ⓓ punish.

23. How would you **contact** a classmate?

    Ⓐ by politely explaining he has made a mistake
    Ⓑ by choosing to be his partner
    Ⓒ by signing up for the same classes
    Ⓓ by calling or e-mailing him

24. Something told in **confidence** should be

    Ⓐ kept secret.
    Ⓑ reported honestly to others.
    Ⓒ immediately suspected.
    Ⓓ reported to the police.

25. When a car **accelerates,** it
    Ⓐ loses power.
    Ⓑ is getting old.
    Ⓒ goes faster.
    Ⓓ should be taken to a mechanic.

26. A bassoon **solo** is performed
    Ⓐ by an orchestra.
    Ⓑ very slowly.
    Ⓒ at the beginning of the program.
    Ⓓ by only one musician.

27. If a table seats a **maximum** of 12 diners, then
    Ⓐ at least 12 diners can sit there.
    Ⓑ no more than 12 people can sit there.
    Ⓒ no less than 12 diners should use the table.
    Ⓓ the 12 diners must share their table with others.

28. What might make you feel **confident** before a math test?
    Ⓐ being weak in math
    Ⓑ sleeping poorly the night before
    Ⓒ studying hard
    Ⓓ skipping breakfast

29. What could be used to **brace** a young lemon tree?
    Ⓐ a hose
    Ⓑ a shovel
    Ⓒ some plant food
    Ⓓ a wooden stake

30. What might make a motorcycle **stall?**
    Ⓐ polishing it
    Ⓑ having it tuned up
    Ⓒ driving at night
    Ⓓ running out of gas

31. A **hangar** is
    Ⓐ a building to shelter planes.
    Ⓑ an object that clothing is hung on.
    Ⓒ a flight school.
    Ⓓ something that holds up something else.

32. Sammy's parents are **anxious.** They often
    Ⓐ sleep very soundly.
    Ⓑ worry about him when he is late.
    Ⓒ plan exciting vacations.
    Ⓓ are very proud of him.

33. You should avoid **contact** with poison oak. In other words, you should not
    Ⓐ grow it.
    Ⓑ look at it.
    Ⓒ touch it.
    Ⓓ eat it.

Name ______________________________ Date ______________

Lesson 12 Test

Find a SYNONYM for each bold word. Then fill in the circle next to your answer.

1. The **tempestuous** debate lasted for three hours.
   - Ⓐ tiresome
   - Ⓑ wild
   - Ⓒ lukewarm
   - Ⓓ confusing

2. Newscasters predicted there'd be a **rebellion** against the new sales tax.
   - Ⓐ opposition
   - Ⓑ agreement
   - Ⓒ law
   - Ⓓ speech

3. The library **restricts** borrowing to five books.
   - Ⓐ prohibits
   - Ⓑ charges
   - Ⓒ limits
   - Ⓓ encourages

4. It **seldom** snows in that part of the country.
   - Ⓐ frequently
   - Ⓑ never
   - Ⓒ repeatedly
   - Ⓓ rarely

5. We are studying Julia de Burgos, a **notable** poet.
   - Ⓐ musical
   - Ⓑ outstanding
   - Ⓒ unknown
   - Ⓓ early

6. Albert Einstein **dedicated** his life to science.
   - Ⓐ sacrificed
   - Ⓑ donated
   - Ⓒ devoted
   - Ⓓ introduced

Find an ANTONYM for each bold word. Then fill in the circle next to your answer.

7. The walk through Redwood National Park **stimulated** Mr. Lew's senses.

   Ⓐ excited
   Ⓑ irritated
   Ⓒ developed
   Ⓓ dulled

8. Rain is **overdue** for this time of the year.

   Ⓐ late
   Ⓑ early
   Ⓒ heavy
   Ⓓ light

9. The school **dictates** the rules in our classroom.

   Ⓐ follows
   Ⓑ invents
   Ⓒ determines
   Ⓓ remembers

10. The speaker was in favor of the **overthrow** of the electoral college.

   Ⓐ expansion
   Ⓑ destruction
   Ⓒ preservation
   Ⓓ revision

Choose the best way to complete each sentence or answer each question. Then fill in the circle next to your answer.

11. Someone who is **convalescing** might be

   Ⓐ enjoying a school vacation.
   Ⓑ getting over the flu.
   Ⓒ having a relaxing weekend.
   Ⓓ taking college courses through the Internet.

12. A **rebel** is

   Ⓐ someone who lives in the Northeast.
   Ⓑ a revolutionary war.
   Ⓒ a government official.
   Ⓓ someone opposed to certain rules.

13. Land that is **dedicated** as a nature preserve is

   Ⓐ named for a nature preserve.
   Ⓑ located near a nature preserve.
   Ⓒ set aside for use as a nature preserve.
   Ⓓ for sale as a nature preserve.

14. Our flashlights failed to **penetrate** the fog. This means that

   Ⓐ we could not throw our flashlights very far.
   Ⓑ the flashlights failed to shine deep through the fog.
   Ⓒ the batteries failed because of the dampness.
   Ⓓ the light shone right through the fog.

15. Which is an example of a **portrait?**

Ⓐ a photograph of Mt. McKinley
Ⓑ a painting of Martha Washington
Ⓒ a miniature sculpture of the Taj Mahal
Ⓓ a biography of Frederick Douglass

16. A **tempest** is

Ⓐ an angry state of mind.
Ⓑ a moderate climate.
Ⓒ a violent storm.
Ⓓ a defeat of the government.

17. Ashleigh had an unusual **upbringing.** This means that

Ⓐ she grew up in unusual circumstances.
Ⓑ she had a way of bringing up unusual ideas.
Ⓒ she had an unusual imagination.
Ⓓ she had an unusual way of bringing up her children.

18. Nicole's questions **exasperated** her brother. He said,

Ⓐ "Let's check the encyclopedia."
Ⓑ "I'm afraid I don't know the answers."
Ⓒ "Just be quiet for a while, will you?"
Ⓓ "Let's figure that out together."

19. What happens when a **dictator** rules a country?

Ⓐ There is a lot of paperwork.
Ⓑ No one else has a say in the government.
Ⓒ The government has more work to do.
Ⓓ Everyone has an equal say in the government.

20. The Mexicans **overthrew** Spain's rule. They

Ⓐ were grateful to be ruled by Spain.
Ⓑ complained about the Spanish.
Ⓒ ended Spain's control over their country.
Ⓓ welcomed Spain's rule.

21. Which of the following could be **dictated?**

Ⓐ the leader of a country
Ⓑ the population of a country
Ⓒ a letter
Ⓓ a computer

22. Which of the following messages is a **restriction?**

Ⓐ "This trail goes to Silver Lake."
Ⓑ "Restrooms can be found at the picnic sites."
Ⓒ "Ask about times for daily nature walks."
Ⓓ "Don't bring dogs into the park."

23. What do **rebellious** children do?

Ⓐ refuse to obey their parents
Ⓑ make a lot of speeches
Ⓒ read books about government
Ⓓ enjoy active games

24. Nick's membership fees are long **overdue.** This means that

Ⓐ they are overpriced.
Ⓑ he did not pay them on time.
Ⓒ it is almost time for them to be paid.
Ⓓ he always pays his dues on time.

25. An **exasperating** situation is one that

Ⓐ makes you feel excited and interested.
Ⓑ makes you want it to last a long time.
Ⓒ puzzles you.
Ⓓ leaves you feeling annoyed and irritated.

26. A park bench was **dedicated** to my aunt. This means that

Ⓐ it was given to her.
Ⓑ it was sold to her.
Ⓒ it has her name on it for all to see.
Ⓓ it was brought by a shipping company.

27. Many colonies **overthrow** their governments overseas. To **overthrow** means

Ⓐ to earn more money.
Ⓑ to ask for better living conditions.
Ⓒ to escape.
Ⓓ to defeat.

28. What can you use to **penetrate** a tomato?

Ⓐ salt
Ⓑ a hot pan
Ⓒ a pizza
Ⓓ a knife

29. The yearbook club **rebelled** against the rules of the bossy president. The club

Ⓐ forgot to pay their dues.
Ⓑ refused to obey the president's rules.
Ⓒ elected a new president.
Ⓓ respected and obeyed their president.

Name ______________________ Date ______________

Lesson 13 Test

Choose the best way to complete each sentence or answer each question. Then fill in the circle next to your answer.

1. Which word is a SYNONYM for **conceal?**

   Ⓐ hide
   Ⓑ show
   Ⓒ admit
   Ⓓ thicken

2. Which of the following could someone **gorge** on?

   Ⓐ a footstool
   Ⓑ a friend
   Ⓒ pancakes
   Ⓓ a movie

3. The noise **tapered** off as Mr. Cardera came in. What does **tapered** mean in this sentence?

   Ⓐ became annoying
   Ⓑ gradually lessened
   Ⓒ stopped immediately
   Ⓓ grew louder

4. A **sluggish** turtle crossed the road. The turtle

   Ⓐ moved like a duck.
   Ⓑ moved with a side-to-side motion.
   Ⓒ dragged itself on its belly like a slug.
   Ⓓ moved slowly.

5. Felix is an **aggressive** cat. What is an ANTONYM for **aggressive?**

   Ⓐ mean
   Ⓑ timid
   Ⓒ home-loving
   Ⓓ sleepy

6. Lions began to gather around the antelope **carcass.** In this sentence, what does **carcass** mean?

   Ⓐ leader
   Ⓑ den
   Ⓒ young animal
   Ⓓ dead body

7. The restaurant can **accommodate** large groups. **Accommodate** means

   Ⓐ feed.
   Ⓑ provide jobs for.
   Ⓒ have room for.
   Ⓓ attract.

8. To **bask** in someone's praise is to

   Ⓐ feel warmed by it.
   Ⓑ listen closely to it.
   Ⓒ remember it.
   Ⓓ ask the person to repeat it.

9. Smog **limits** the visibility in Los Angeles. This means that

   Ⓐ breathing is difficult in Los Angeles.
   Ⓑ the smog makes it hard to see distant objects.
   Ⓒ the smog keeps people indoors sometimes.
   Ⓓ the poor air has limited the growth of the city.

10. What can someone do with a **taper?**

   Ⓐ seal a package
   Ⓑ record a song
   Ⓒ use it to control the flow of water
   Ⓓ light a room

11. What might make you **flail** your arms?

   Ⓐ taking a shower
   Ⓑ being puzzled
   Ⓒ being surrounded by mosquitoes
   Ⓓ being hot

12. What could make a pond **ripple?**

   Ⓐ bright sunlight
   Ⓑ a long hot spell
   Ⓒ throwing a pebble into it
   Ⓓ too many plants growing in it

13. Where would a lizard be likely to **bask?**

   Ⓐ in the shade of leaves
   Ⓑ on a sunny rock
   Ⓒ under a rock where insects live
   Ⓓ in a gap under a cool rock

14. Where might you be most likely to find a **gorge?**

   Ⓐ in a rocky, mountainous area
   Ⓑ on a prairie
   Ⓒ in the ocean
   Ⓓ on a sandy beach

15. Your hosts will **accommodate** you to the best of their ability. What does **accommodate** mean in this sentence?

   Ⓐ ignore you
   Ⓑ ask you to leave
   Ⓒ refer you to a hotel to stay in
   Ⓓ do favors for you

16. Amber is an **aggressive** chess player. She

   Ⓐ is a new player.
   Ⓑ is a bad player.
   Ⓒ is a bold player.
   Ⓓ is the best player in the country.

17. Something that is barely **visible** is

   Ⓐ difficult to hear.
   Ⓑ difficult to smell.
   Ⓒ difficult to understand.
   Ⓓ difficult to see.

18. Which of the following **protrudes** from a door?

   Ⓐ a hinge
   Ⓑ a peephole
   Ⓒ a doorknob
   Ⓓ a visitor

19. What is an ANTONYM for **sluggish?**

Ⓐ dry
Ⓑ lively
Ⓒ attractive
Ⓓ slow

20. To **slither** is to move like

Ⓐ a rhinoceros.
Ⓑ a snake.
Ⓒ a seagull.
Ⓓ a rabbit.

21. Marina had a **morsel** of cake. Which of the following means the same as a **morsel?**

Ⓐ a small piece
Ⓑ a large piece
Ⓒ a regular serving
Ⓓ an entire cake

22. Mr. Borges is looking for pants that **taper.** What kind of pants will he be likely to buy?

Ⓐ pants that he can wear to the gym
Ⓑ pants that have a designer label
Ⓒ pants that are less wide at the ankles than the thigh
Ⓓ pants that are very wide throughout

23. The insect's leaf-like wings decrease its **visibility.** This means that it

Ⓐ has trouble flying.
Ⓑ is less tasty to birds.
Ⓒ is less able to hide itself.
Ⓓ is hard to spot.

24. How do **ripples** move on a pond?

Ⓐ in a spiral, like a tornado
Ⓑ gently, making shallow waves
Ⓒ all over, in an unordered fashion
Ⓓ fiercely, like ocean waves

25. Which of the following animals has a **snout?**

Ⓐ a fish
Ⓑ an elephant
Ⓒ a pig
Ⓓ an eagle

Name ______________________________ Date ______________

Lesson 14 Test

Find a SYNONYM for each bold word. Then fill in the circle next to your answer.

1. The north gate gives you **access** to the zoo.

   Ⓐ view
   Ⓑ entry
   Ⓒ shortcut
   Ⓓ directions

2. Two of his classmates **taunted** the new student.

   Ⓐ helped
   Ⓑ jeered
   Ⓒ greeted
   Ⓓ accompanied

3. Height is actually not a **requirement** for professional basketball players.

   Ⓐ necessity
   Ⓑ advantage
   Ⓒ compensation
   Ⓓ feature

4. The proposed contract **provides** good health coverage.

   Ⓐ lacks
   Ⓑ describes
   Ⓒ supplies
   Ⓓ abolishes

5. Though she'd been a **delicate** child, Rebekkah became a star athlete.

   Ⓐ lazy
   Ⓑ serious
   Ⓒ strong
   Ⓓ weak

6. A **brilliant** light was visible at the bridge.

   Ⓐ dim
   Ⓑ weak
   Ⓒ bright
   Ⓓ flickering

Find an ANTONYM for each bold word. Then fill in the circle next to your answer.

7. The children grew more **boisterous** as the evening passed.

Ⓐ hungry
Ⓑ quiet
Ⓒ lively
Ⓓ cheerful

8. Huckleberry Finn was an **idle** boy.

Ⓐ busy
Ⓑ smart
Ⓒ unsatisfactory
Ⓓ disliked

9. Johnny Appleseed traveled through the **wilderness** spreading seeds.

Ⓐ canyons
Ⓑ mountains
Ⓒ foothills
Ⓓ city

10. Malcolm's parents raised him to be **tolerant.**

Ⓐ unhealthy
Ⓑ patient
Ⓒ ashamed
Ⓓ narrow-minded

11. Of course, Jones Beach is **accessible** from the highway.

Ⓐ hidden
Ⓑ visible
Ⓒ unreachable
Ⓓ approachable

12. The street was **illuminated** for the festival.

Ⓐ undecorated
Ⓑ dirtied
Ⓒ deserted
Ⓓ darkened

Choose the best way to complete each sentence or answer each question. Then fill in the circle next to your answer.

13. Which two items are easiest to **associate?**

Ⓐ elevators and windows
Ⓑ shoes and t-shirts
Ⓒ peanut butter and jelly
Ⓓ fish and deer

14. Uncle Saul commented on Kyle's **transformation.** He said,

Ⓐ "Your posture needs improving."
Ⓑ "How you've changed since I last saw you!"
Ⓒ "This is a lovely story, Kyle."
Ⓓ "I hear that you have changed schools."

15. **Employ** common sense when riding your bike. In this sentence, **employ** means

    Ⓐ use.
    Ⓑ assign.
    Ⓒ conquer.
    Ⓓ cultivate.

16. The plane **idled** on the runway. This means that

    Ⓐ it was slowly moving forward for take-off.
    Ⓑ its engine was not running, and it was doing nothing.
    Ⓒ its engine was running, but it was not moving.
    Ⓓ it was gently touching down on the runway.

17. A worker's **associates** are

    Ⓐ previous bosses.
    Ⓑ only workers higher in rank.
    Ⓒ people with whom he works closely.
    Ⓓ the tasks he performs daily.

18. If you have **access** to a tennis court, you

    Ⓐ live behind it.
    Ⓑ are free to use it when you like.
    Ⓒ must get permission to use it.
    Ⓓ can take public transportation to it.

19. Which of the following is most **delicate?**

    Ⓐ a cobweb
    Ⓑ a chair
    Ⓒ a good book
    Ⓓ a peacock

20. Can someone **illuminate** me about this article? In this sentence, **illuminate** means

    Ⓐ shine a lamp on the page.
    Ⓑ make drawings to go with it.
    Ⓒ make its meaning clear to me.
    Ⓓ make a copy of it.

21. If you **require** a library card, you

    Ⓐ get one.
    Ⓑ need one.
    Ⓒ stop using one.
    Ⓓ ask questions about one.

22. Which of the following is a **taunt?**

    Ⓐ "Don't swing if the pitch is low!"
    Ⓑ "You're out!"
    Ⓒ "You can't hit the ball to save your life!"
    Ⓓ "Run for home!"

23. It is often difficult, but Ms. Putnam always **tolerates** her noisy neighbors. What does **tolerate** mean in this sentence?

    Ⓐ adores them
    Ⓑ gives them a lecture
    Ⓒ evades them
    Ⓓ puts up with them

24. To **provide** lunch is to

    Ⓐ supply it.
    Ⓑ plan it.
    Ⓒ purchase it.
    Ⓓ break it up into parts.

25. Malik **associates** with artists. This means that he

    Ⓐ thinks of himself as an artist.
    Ⓑ spends time with artists.
    Ⓒ sometimes does business with artists.
    Ⓓ works across the street from some artists.

26. We **idled** in the back yard all afternoon. This means that we

    Ⓐ took care of small chores.
    Ⓑ relaxed and did nothing.
    Ⓒ repaired a car.
    Ⓓ dug up weeds.

27. A **delicate** situation calls for someone to

    Ⓐ care for a sick person.
    Ⓑ move brittle objects.
    Ⓒ act immediately.
    Ⓓ act with care and skill.

28. Which of the following can **employ** people?

    Ⓐ an insult
    Ⓑ a challenge
    Ⓒ a shop
    Ⓓ a television

29. A **brilliant** idea is

    Ⓐ reasonable.
    Ⓑ clever.
    Ⓒ foolhardy.
    Ⓓ confusing.

30. The couple **required** a quiet hotel. This means that they

    Ⓐ demanded a quiet hotel.
    Ⓑ reserved rooms in a quiet hotel.
    Ⓒ stayed in a quiet hotel.
    Ⓓ ran a quiet hotel.

31. What is an example of a **decade?**

    Ⓐ 1800–1900
    Ⓑ 1950–2000
    Ⓒ 500 B.C.E.
    Ⓓ 1920–1930

32. Ben **transformed** the toy robot into a spacecraft. A SYNONYM for **transformed** is

    Ⓐ crashed.
    Ⓑ changed.
    Ⓒ moved.
    Ⓓ fitted.

Name ______________________ Date ____________

Lesson 15 Test

Choose the best way to complete each sentence or answer each question. Then fill in the circle next to your answer.

1. A SYNONYM for **immense** is

   Ⓐ strong.
   Ⓑ deep.
   Ⓒ gigantic.
   Ⓓ extinct.

2. Jon is a **minor.** This means that

   Ⓐ he works in a mine.
   Ⓑ he is not yet an adult.
   Ⓒ he is an army officer.
   Ⓓ he writes music.

3. As a tree **petrifies,** its

   Ⓐ growth slows down.
   Ⓑ leaves begin to uncurl.
   Ⓒ plant matter is replaced by stone.
   Ⓓ roots grow deeper into the earth.

4. Mr. Olsen is **prone** to sunburns. This means that

   Ⓐ he gets sunburns only when he lies on his stomach.
   Ⓑ he rarely gets sunburns.
   Ⓒ he is accustomed to sunburns.
   Ⓓ he is likely to get sunburns.

5. One SYNONYM for **major** is

   Ⓐ accurate.
   Ⓑ important.
   Ⓒ skillful.
   Ⓓ vast.

6. The car gave a quick **lurch.** A **lurch** is

   Ⓐ a noise.
   Ⓑ a crash.
   Ⓒ a jerk.
   Ⓓ a shiver.

7. Baby Luis **toppled** Donna's pile of blocks. What did Luis do?

   Ⓐ He carefully piled the blocks up.
   Ⓑ He helped Donna build the pile.
   Ⓒ He stacked the pile too high.
   Ⓓ He pushed Donna's pile over.

8. The director's words were **intense.** This means that her words

   Ⓐ showed strong feelings.
   Ⓑ were aggressive.
   Ⓒ were formal.
   Ⓓ filled the room.

9. Which of the following is a natural **disaster?**
   Ⓐ the summertime
   Ⓑ an earthquake
   Ⓒ a national park
   Ⓓ a breezy day

10. If an audience is **sparse,** that means that
   Ⓐ it is reluctant to leave.
   Ⓑ it is completely involved in the play.
   Ⓒ the performers are doing a good job.
   Ⓓ there are many empty seats in the theater.

11. You might **flee** your classroom if
   Ⓐ there is a fire drill.
   Ⓑ it is the end of the day.
   Ⓒ you need to use the bathroom.
   Ⓓ you are going to lunch.

12. Where are you most likely to meet a **major?**
   Ⓐ on an army base
   Ⓑ in elementary school
   Ⓒ in a city hall
   Ⓓ on a football field

13. Which of the following statements is a **prediction?**
   Ⓐ "I had a terrible weekend."
   Ⓑ "It's going to rain this weekend."
   Ⓒ "Emile left me behind."
   Ⓓ "I didn't really cause the accident."

14. A **minor** problem might be
   Ⓐ losing your job.
   Ⓑ running out of milk.
   Ⓒ crashing your car.
   Ⓓ breaking your leg.

15. An ANTONYM for **investigate** is
   Ⓐ search.
   Ⓑ question.
   Ⓒ distract.
   Ⓓ ignore.

16. The **intensity** of the fire made us
   Ⓐ put more wood on it.
   Ⓑ comment on its size.
   Ⓒ move away from the heat.
   Ⓓ feel chilly.

17. Samantha **fractured** the sculpture she made in art class. Samantha
   Ⓐ broke the sculpture.
   Ⓑ gave the sculpture as a gift.
   Ⓒ was proud of the sculpture.
   Ⓓ lost the sculpture.

18. When the kingdom was **toppled,** the king and queen
   Ⓐ became very rich.
   Ⓑ called for a celebration.
   Ⓒ lost all their powers.
   Ⓓ became dictators.

19. Yolanda was absolutely **petrified** by the movie. What kind of movie was Yolanda probably watching?

Ⓐ a comedy
Ⓑ a horror movie
Ⓒ an action movie
Ⓓ a foreign movie

20. Someone choosing a **major** in college might choose

Ⓐ her best friend.
Ⓑ softball.
Ⓒ mathematics.
Ⓓ the college her mother went to.

21. If you **predict** a victory for your team, you are

Ⓐ worried about your team's chances of winning.
Ⓑ longing for your team to win.
Ⓒ guessing that your team will win.
Ⓓ writing about a winning game.

22. Which is the opposite of an **urban** area?

Ⓐ downtown
Ⓑ a shopping mall
Ⓒ a harbor
Ⓓ the countryside

23. What might have a **fracture** in it?

Ⓐ a salad
Ⓑ a sock
Ⓒ a cement sidewalk
Ⓓ a pile of sand

24. Grandfather Rasmussen's hair was **sparse.** A SYNONYM for **sparse** is

Ⓐ gray.
Ⓑ thin.
Ⓒ shaggy.
Ⓓ tidy.

25. Dominic used an **intense** red in his painting. What kind of color was he using?

Ⓐ a pinkish-orange
Ⓑ a reddish-brown
Ⓒ a strong, bright red
Ⓓ a dark, dull red

26. When the ferry **lurched** forward, I was

Ⓐ surprised by its slowness.
Ⓑ amazed at its speed.
Ⓒ almost thrown out of my seat.
Ⓓ worried that we would be late.

27. Someone in a **prone** position is

Ⓐ lying facedown.
Ⓑ absolutely vertical.
Ⓒ huddled.
Ⓓ sitting in a chair.

28. Neville **majored** in history. This means that

Ⓐ he failed his history tests.
Ⓑ he did well on his history tests.
Ⓒ he was not interested in history.
Ⓓ history was his main subject in college.

29. The **disastrous** voyage ended

    Ⓐ in a tropical place.
    Ⓑ in a shipwreck.
    Ⓒ with a party on board the ship.
    Ⓓ a day later than was planned.

30. The passengers **fled** the ship when

    Ⓐ they docked in the harbor.
    Ⓑ the workday ended.
    Ⓒ they hit an iceberg.
    Ⓓ the fishing boats arrived.

31. It took **immense** self-control to be quiet during the ceremony. **Immense** means

    Ⓐ a great deal of.
    Ⓑ very little.
    Ⓒ anxious.
    Ⓓ confident.

Name ______________________ Date ______________

Lesson 16 Test

Find a SYNONYM for each bold word. Then fill in the circle next to your answer.

1. The shortage of bread caused public **riots.**

   Ⓐ hunger
   Ⓑ disorder
   Ⓒ despair
   Ⓓ complaints

2. War was **proclaimed** in 1941.

   Ⓐ abolished
   Ⓑ conquered
   Ⓒ announced
   Ⓓ ended

3. Erik **pardoned** his sister for her lateness.

   Ⓐ nagged
   Ⓑ blamed
   Ⓒ lectured
   Ⓓ forgave

4. All our **kin** will be at the picnic.

   Ⓐ relatives
   Ⓑ friends
   Ⓒ neighbors
   Ⓓ community

5. The movers **hoisted** the piano to the second floor.

   Ⓐ pushed
   Ⓑ lowered
   Ⓒ dropped
   Ⓓ lifted

6. Justin **dominated** every conversation.

   Ⓐ whined
   Ⓑ surrendered
   Ⓒ shouted
   Ⓓ controlled

7. Dermott **intercepted** his sister's letter.

   Ⓐ read
   Ⓑ seized
   Ⓒ translated
   Ⓓ preserved

Find an ANTONYM for each bold word. Then fill in the circle next to your answer.

8. Ms. Yee is the **former** board president.

Ⓐ present
Ⓑ correct
Ⓒ previous
Ⓓ elected

9. Stacia's remarks **provoked** her brother.

Ⓐ annoyed
Ⓑ calmed
Ⓒ exasperated
Ⓓ forgave

10. William **assumes** that Kayla will help him with his homework.

Ⓐ doubts
Ⓑ promises
Ⓒ understands
Ⓓ establishes

11. Of trains and airplanes, I prefer riding in the **former.**

Ⓐ faster
Ⓑ slower
Ⓒ first
Ⓓ last

Choose the best way to complete each sentence or answer each question. Then fill in the circle next to your answer.

12. Which of the following **reigns?**

Ⓐ a horse
Ⓑ a president
Ⓒ a queen
Ⓓ dark clouds

13. A dragon was the **guardian** of the cave. The dragon

Ⓐ protected the cave.
Ⓑ lived in the cave.
Ⓒ took care of its baby dragons in the cave.
Ⓓ never left the cave for any reason.

14. Fiona received a **pardon** from the president even though

Ⓐ she was employed by the government.
Ⓑ she had no prior offenses.
Ⓒ she was innocent.
Ⓓ she was guilty.

15. Jackson Pollock's paintings are a **riot** of color and shapes. His paintings are probably

Ⓐ very small.
Ⓑ very orderly and precise.
Ⓒ blank or sparse.
Ⓓ seemingly wild and disordered.

16. At the awards ceremony, the boys **assumed** the manners of fine gentlemen. This means that they

Ⓐ observed the manners of fine gentlemen.
Ⓑ jeered at the manners of fine gentlemen.
Ⓒ were actually fine gentlemen.
Ⓓ pretended they were fine gentlemen.

17. Ty's **next of kin** is most likely to be

Ⓐ his best friend.
Ⓑ his school principal.
Ⓒ his parent.
Ⓓ his stepbrother.

18. A **guardian** is someone who

Ⓐ patrols a shopping mall.
Ⓑ legally acts as a parent.
Ⓒ works in a jail.
Ⓓ looks after someone's estate.

19. A **hoist** is used to

Ⓐ welcome people to an event.
Ⓑ lift heavy objects.
Ⓒ commit a robbery.
Ⓓ keep a horse from straying.

20. The article **provoked** a lively discussion on the Middle East. This means that

Ⓐ it brought about a discussion.
Ⓑ it analyzed previous discussions.
Ⓒ it stopped further discussion.
Ⓓ it angered the people who were already discussing.

21. A **jubilee** celebration is most likely to take place

Ⓐ on the day after a holiday.
Ⓑ on New Year's Day.
Ⓒ on the fiftieth anniversary of an event.
Ⓓ on someone's sixtieth birthday.

22. Sunni Ali Ber **reigned** over his small kingdom in Western Africa for twenty-eight years. For twenty-eight years, Sunni Ali Ber

Ⓐ lived in the kingdom.
Ⓑ was not allowed in the kingdom.
Ⓒ fought with the kingdom.
Ⓓ ruled the kingdom.

23. The Australian desert is **dominated** by snakes and lizards. This means that

Ⓐ snakes and lizards are always preyed upon in the Australian desert.
Ⓑ snakes and lizards are found only in the Australian desert.
Ⓒ there are very many snakes and lizards in the Australian desert.
Ⓓ there are very few snakes and lizards in the Australian desert.

24. To **abdicate** the presidency is to

Ⓐ long for it.
Ⓑ try to be elected to it.
Ⓒ give it up.
Ⓓ be awarded it.

25. Someone who is **kin** to you is

Ⓐ tolerant.

Ⓑ good-hearted.

Ⓒ helpful to you.

Ⓓ related to you.

26. Because the president had **pardoned** him, the prisoner

Ⓐ was severely punished.

Ⓑ was given another trial.

Ⓒ was set free.

Ⓓ was pronounced not guilty.

27. When Jason **assumed** the role of secretary, he

Ⓐ challenged the secretary.

Ⓑ took on the secretary's duties.

Ⓒ refused to be the secretary anymore.

Ⓓ wondered if the group needed a secretary.

28. If a film has a **provocative** ending, the ending

Ⓐ makes the audience think.

Ⓑ is a disappointment.

Ⓒ bores the audience.

Ⓓ is easy to predict.

29. When taxes were raised, the people **rioted. Rioted** means

Ⓐ wrote letters of complaint.

Ⓑ shouted angrily in the streets.

Ⓒ overthrew the government.

Ⓓ lost hope.

30. High spirits **reign** during the annual carnival. **Reign** means

Ⓐ are dampened.

Ⓑ ride in a parade.

Ⓒ are widespread.

Ⓓ rebel.

31. Brandon **bungled** the job and had to do it again. This means that he

Ⓐ forgot to do the job.

Ⓑ stole the job from a friend.

Ⓒ told everyone what a hateful job it was.

Ⓓ did not do a skillful job.

Name ______________________ Date ____________

Test

Find a SYNONYM for each bold word. Then fill in the circle next to your answer.

1. Antonio has a **fertile** mind.
   Ⓐ quick
   Ⓑ inventive
   Ⓒ restless
   Ⓓ forgetful

2. Will Kevin **revert** to his old habits?
   Ⓐ return
   Ⓑ mention
   Ⓒ change
   Ⓓ regret

3. Much of the tundra is **barren** land.
   Ⓐ rocky
   Ⓑ icy
   Ⓒ bare
   Ⓓ broad

4. Westward **expansion** finally reached the Pacific coast.
   Ⓐ transportation
   Ⓑ exploration
   Ⓒ trail-building
   Ⓓ growth

5. The leaves **withered** on the grape vine.
   Ⓐ uncurled
   Ⓑ sprouted
   Ⓒ dried
   Ⓓ trembled

Find an ANTONYM for each bold word. Then fill in the circle next to your answer.

6. Near-sightedness is a very common **affliction.**
   Ⓐ problem
   Ⓑ trait
   Ⓒ responsibility
   Ⓓ benefit

7. The museum was showing an exhibit on **primitive** art.
   Ⓐ old-fashioned
   Ⓑ modern
   Ⓒ ugly
   Ⓓ unexciting

8. Heavy rains **eroded** the adobe walls.

   Ⓐ stained
   Ⓑ beat
   Ⓒ painted
   Ⓓ repaired

9. Heat **expands** the air in a hot-air balloon.

   Ⓐ explodes
   Ⓑ enlarges
   Ⓒ darkens
   Ⓓ shrinks

10. The family survived many years of **famine.**

   Ⓐ rioting
   Ⓑ toil
   Ⓒ plenty
   Ⓓ ease

Choose the best way to complete each sentence or answer each question. Then fill in the circle next to your answer.

11. Lee's parents were **refugees** from Bosnia. His parents

   Ⓐ were soldiers in their country.
   Ⓑ were farmers in their country.
   Ⓒ left their country seeking protection.
   Ⓓ were on vacation from their country.

12. Advin's parents found **refuge** in Canada. Refuge means

   Ⓐ other relatives.
   Ⓑ well-paying jobs.
   Ⓒ a protected place to live.
   Ⓓ rejection.

13. Which of the following can be **pastured?**

   Ⓐ pencils
   Ⓑ goats
   Ⓒ milk
   Ⓓ walls

14. Which of these places is probably the least **fertile?**

   Ⓐ a farm
   Ⓑ a meadow
   Ⓒ a desert
   Ⓓ a garden

15. In **oases,** you will find

Ⓐ shopping malls.
Ⓑ wells or springs.
Ⓒ mountains.
Ⓓ gorges.

16. The old emperor was **afflicted** with

Ⓐ a treasure house full of gold.
Ⓑ his favorite sister.
Ⓒ two selfish daughters.
Ⓓ a vast kingdom.

17. What happens during a **drought?**

Ⓐ Rivers dry up.
Ⓑ Hurricanes come in from the sea.
Ⓒ People take vacations.
Ⓓ Young men become soldiers.

18. What is an effect of **erosion?**

Ⓐ The land wears away.
Ⓑ Skyscrapers are built.
Ⓒ Trade between nations increases.
Ⓓ Temperatures throughout the world increase.

19. The pasture was **teeming** with

Ⓐ four cows.
Ⓑ hundreds of field mice.
Ⓒ two loud roosters.
Ⓓ an old apple tree.

20. What can fruit salad **consist** of?

Ⓐ dessert
Ⓑ someone's only snack
Ⓒ bananas, cherries, and peaches
Ⓓ whipped cream

21. A **fertile** hamster is one that

Ⓐ can produce offspring.
Ⓑ is afraid of people.
Ⓒ eats a lot of food.
Ⓓ has not been tamed.

22. Which is another word for a **pasture?**

Ⓐ river
Ⓑ farm
Ⓒ meadow
Ⓓ fruit

23. The teacher told Jasmine to **expand** upon her idea. What should Jasmine do?

Ⓐ debate her idea with someone else
Ⓑ give more information about her idea
Ⓒ write a story about her idea
Ⓓ forget about her idea

24. A good **refuge** from the sun and heat is

Ⓐ a playground.
Ⓑ the backyard.
Ⓒ a cool library.
Ⓓ the beach.

25. The area outside of an **oasis** is

Ⓐ thickly settled.
Ⓑ farm land.
Ⓒ tropical.
Ⓓ dry.

26. Dad and Henri built a very **primitive** tree house. In this sentence, **primitive** means

Ⓐ small.
Ⓑ old.
Ⓒ crude.
Ⓓ ancient.

Name ______________________ Date ______________

Lesson 18 Test

Find a SYNONYM for each bold word. Then fill in the circle next to your answer.

1. She fixed a **meager** breakfast.

   Ⓐ edible
   Ⓑ bland
   Ⓒ insufficient
   Ⓓ delicious

2. Ana was **animated** during the conversation.

   Ⓐ silent
   Ⓑ thoughtful
   Ⓒ lively
   Ⓓ offended

3. It was a **somber** occasion for the Ruiz family.

   Ⓐ sad
   Ⓑ unforgettable
   Ⓒ joyous
   Ⓓ unusual

4. This computer is now **obsolete.**

   Ⓐ repaired
   Ⓑ expensive
   Ⓒ portable
   Ⓓ outdated

5. Jacob met the vice president at a **subsequent** meeting.

   Ⓐ earlier
   Ⓑ later
   Ⓒ important
   Ⓓ summit

6. She remembered her **vow** to her brother.

   Ⓐ unkindness
   Ⓑ promise
   Ⓒ insult
   Ⓓ loan

7. Jules **declined** the invitation to the ballet.

   Ⓐ sent
   Ⓑ accepted
   Ⓒ forgot
   Ⓓ refused

Find an ANTONYM for each bold word. Then fill in the circle next to your answer.

8. Gillian's **mischief** made it difficult to find a babysitter.

   Ⓐ silence
   Ⓑ carefulness
   Ⓒ helpfulness
   Ⓓ patience

9. Dan **convinced** his sister to sign up for the football team.

   Ⓐ ignored
   Ⓑ persuaded
   Ⓒ discouraged
   Ⓓ distracted

10. The trapeze act was **sensational.**

   Ⓐ ordinary
   Ⓑ thrilling
   Ⓒ inventive
   Ⓓ makeshift

11. Don't **betray** Lula's hiding place.

   Ⓐ hunt
   Ⓑ conceal
   Ⓒ discover
   Ⓓ reveal

12. The road **declined** just beyond the bridge.

   Ⓐ curved
   Ⓑ widened
   Ⓒ started
   Ⓓ rose

13. The museum **retained** a scientist and a curator.

   Ⓐ showed
   Ⓑ fired
   Ⓒ hired
   Ⓓ used

Choose the best way to complete each sentence or answer each question. Then fill in the circle next to your answer.

14. You might have to **negotiate** your way if you are

   Ⓐ trying to cross a crowded city street.
   Ⓑ visiting your mother at work.
   Ⓒ waiting in line to see a movie.
   Ⓓ swimming in an empty pool.

15. Her health **declined** when she changed her diet. **Declined** means

   Ⓐ went up and down.
   Ⓑ became worse.
   Ⓒ stayed the same.
   Ⓓ improved.

16. A **mischievous** person is

Ⓐ hostile to strangers.
Ⓑ boisterous but tired.
Ⓒ naughty but playful.
Ⓓ loud and aggressive.

17. The movie is a **sensation!** All the reviews say,

Ⓐ "Don't waste your time going."
Ⓑ "Dress warmly because the theater's unheated."
Ⓒ "The book was better."
Ⓓ "It's the best movie of the year!"

18. Filmmakers use new technology to make ordinary figures seem **animated.** This means that the figures

Ⓐ seem much larger than they are.
Ⓑ are very colorful.
Ⓒ move as if they were alive.
Ⓓ are three-dimensional.

19. Lee **negotiated** with his mother. The results were that

Ⓐ he was grounded for a month.
Ⓑ his grades went down.
Ⓒ he got a higher allowance in exchange for doing more chores.
Ⓓ he refused to go to school for a week.

20. Mexico **retained** Baja California. This means that Mexico

Ⓐ gave the area to another country.
Ⓑ sold the area to another country.
Ⓒ took over the area.
Ⓓ kept possession of the area.

21. The **sensational** headline announced,

Ⓐ "More Rain Due This Week."
Ⓑ "Buses Add More Routes."
Ⓒ "Noted Author to Speak at Book Shop."
Ⓓ "Giant Gorilla Climbs Chicago Skyscraper."

22. An example of making **mischief** is

Ⓐ forgetting to wear your coat.
Ⓑ spreading unkind and untrue gossip.
Ⓒ sharing your notes with a classmate.
Ⓓ accidentally spilling your chocolate milk.

23. The path led from the bright, cheerful meadow into the **somber** shade of the forest. In this sentence, **somber** means

Ⓐ hot and steamy.
Ⓑ sweet-smelling.
Ⓒ dark and gloomy.
Ⓓ quiet and peaceful.

24. Benedict Arnold **betrayed** his country when he

    Ⓐ became a soldier in its army.
    Ⓑ fought off the enemy in several important battles.
    Ⓒ became a citizen.
    Ⓓ sold secrets to the enemy.

25. A **decline** in sales is

    Ⓐ a temporary rise in sales.
    Ⓑ a decrease in sales.
    Ⓒ an increase in sales.
    Ⓓ an expansion of sales.

26. Rosie's **hilarious** story made us

    Ⓐ admire what she had been through.
    Ⓑ reluctant to speak.
    Ⓒ laugh out loud.
    Ⓓ cry quietly.

27. Tyler **vowed** to change his exercise habits. **Vowed** means

    Ⓐ promised.
    Ⓑ refused.
    Ⓒ tried.
    Ⓓ expected.

28. What could produce an unpleasant **sensation?**

    Ⓐ imagining a hot day
    Ⓑ stepping on a slug while barefoot
    Ⓒ having an argument with your brother
    Ⓓ forgetting to do your homework

29. What could be a **likeness** of Martin Luther King Jr.?

    Ⓐ a portrait of Martin Luther King Jr.
    Ⓑ an article about Martin Luther King Jr.
    Ⓒ a friend of Martin Luther King Jr.
    Ⓓ a speech given by Martin Luther King Jr.

30. The children got into **mischief** and

    Ⓐ were not hungry at lunch time.
    Ⓑ played hide-and-seek for half an hour.
    Ⓒ dressed the dog in the baby's clothes.
    Ⓓ had to take a bath.

31. The **decline** of the Anasazi civilization was thought to be because of problems with the turquoise trade. In this sentence, **decline** means

    Ⓐ expansion.
    Ⓑ aggression.
    Ⓒ blooming.
    Ⓓ weakening.

Name ______________________ Date ____________

Test

Find a SYNONYM for each bold word. Then fill in the circle next to your answer.

1. How many people **perished** in the Civil War?

   Ⓐ fought
   Ⓑ enlisted
   Ⓒ died
   Ⓓ starved

2. The riots were a **prelude** to the revolution.

   Ⓐ conclusion
   Ⓑ symptom
   Ⓒ introduction
   Ⓓ disadvantage

3. The explorers came upon a **stupendous** waterfall.

   Ⓐ amazing
   Ⓑ concealed
   Ⓒ tall
   Ⓓ dangerous

4. I felt a **tremor** of nervousness as I stepped onto the stage.

   Ⓐ lack
   Ⓑ decrease
   Ⓒ increase
   Ⓓ shiver

5. The economy is **dormant** now.

   Ⓐ prosperous
   Ⓑ inactive
   Ⓒ expanding
   Ⓓ convalescing

6. Dr. Kim and her students **excavated** the site.

   Ⓐ dug
   Ⓑ removed
   Ⓒ studied
   Ⓓ concealed

Find an ANTONYM for each bold word. Then fill in the circle next to your answer.

7. Excelsior Geyser produces 4,000 gallons of **scalding** water each minute.

   Ⓐ hot
   Ⓑ icy
   Ⓒ salty
   Ⓓ dirty

8. It's likely that Corey will be **expelled** from school.

   Ⓐ bored
   Ⓑ admitted
   Ⓒ prohibited
   Ⓓ rewarded

9. Erika is a **painstaking** carpenter.

   Ⓐ healthy
   Ⓑ generous
   Ⓒ careless
   Ⓓ careful

10. Brian writes **elegant** prose.

   Ⓐ unconvincing
   Ⓑ sloppy
   Ⓒ complicated
   Ⓓ superior

Choose the best way to complete each sentence or answer each question. Then fill in the circle next to your answer.

11. He encountered the **fumes** of

   Ⓐ the garden.
   Ⓑ the boiling water.
   Ⓒ the burning rubber.
   Ⓓ his angry sister.

12. To find out the squirrel **population** of your neighborhood, you should

   Ⓐ find out what draws them there.
   Ⓑ find a means of counting them.
   Ⓒ find out what they are eating.
   Ⓓ identify their habits.

13. The bears are **dormant** now. They will

   Ⓐ attack anyone who comes near.
   Ⓑ ignore you as long as you stay out of their way.
   Ⓒ take a rest after they have stopped eating.
   Ⓓ stay in a sleeplike state until spring.

14. When we pour the **molten** syrup in the mold, it will

   Ⓐ cool and harden.
   Ⓑ soon become liquid.
   Ⓒ freeze our hands if we touch it.
   Ⓓ resemble sand.

15. What did scientists do to **excavate** Pompeii?

    Ⓐ wrote about its history
    Ⓑ uncovered its buried ruins
    Ⓒ took a tour
    Ⓓ moved there and settled

16. The baby **expelled** a mouthful of strained peas. In this sentence, **expelled** means

    Ⓐ spit out.
    Ⓑ swallowed.
    Ⓒ chewed slowly.
    Ⓓ enjoyed.

17. **Suffocation** is

    Ⓐ being in a sleeplike state.
    Ⓑ suffering from pain.
    Ⓒ dying for lack of air.
    Ⓓ being pleased with something.

18. The geyser **erupted,** and

    Ⓐ a mist floated over it.
    Ⓑ the earth was illuminated.
    Ⓒ a column of steaming water burst up.
    Ⓓ snow began to fall.

19. That **excavation** is the site of the future community pool. **Excavation** means

    Ⓐ marked-off area.
    Ⓑ platform.
    Ⓒ place where there are ruins.
    Ⓓ dug-out area.

20. Where are you most likely to hear a **prelude?**

    Ⓐ at a baseball game
    Ⓑ in a movie theater
    Ⓒ at a concert
    Ⓓ in a shopping mall

21. Oregon is not as heavily **populated** as California. This means that

    Ⓐ Oregon is not an attractive place to live.
    Ⓑ fewer people live in Oregon.
    Ⓒ the air is purer in Oregon.
    Ⓓ Oregon does not have as much wildlife as California.

22. Brittany was **scalded** when she

    Ⓐ heard the insult.
    Ⓑ said those unpleasant things.
    Ⓒ spilled hot tea on her hand.
    Ⓓ was late to class.

23. Someone is most likely to **fume** over

    Ⓐ steak for dinner.
    Ⓑ a hilarious joke.
    Ⓒ a thoughtful question.
    Ⓓ a mean remark.

24. To keep the fireflies he had captured from **suffocating,** Tito

    Ⓐ gave them plenty of water.
    Ⓑ punched air holes in their container.
    Ⓒ fed them regularly.
    Ⓓ put the container in a dark room.

25. The **population** of a city refers to

Ⓐ the number of people living in it.
Ⓑ the problems that it has.
Ⓒ the animals living in it.
Ⓓ the wealth of its citizens.

26. The **eruption** of applause surprised the singer. What does **eruption** mean in this sentence?

Ⓐ steady stream
Ⓑ abrupt end
Ⓒ sudden burst
Ⓓ puny amount

Name ______________________ Date ______________

Lesson 20 Test

Find a SYNONYM for each bold word. Then fill in the circle next to your answer.

1. Are you going to **comply** with the rules of the game?

   Ⓐ tamper
   Ⓑ argue
   Ⓒ obey
   Ⓓ leave

2. Vincent's **distress** could be seen on his face.

   Ⓐ jubilation
   Ⓑ sorrow
   Ⓒ anger
   Ⓓ boredom

3. The strange **encounter** took place at the bank.

   Ⓐ meeting
   Ⓑ robbery
   Ⓒ deposit
   Ⓓ discovery

4. The children understood the **moral** of the fable.

   Ⓐ plot
   Ⓑ setting
   Ⓒ lesson
   Ⓓ characters

5. His brother **ridiculed** him for buying the old bicycle.

   Ⓐ congratulated
   Ⓑ envied
   Ⓒ lectured
   Ⓓ taunted

6. Their conversation left Lola **indignant.**

   Ⓐ illuminated
   Ⓑ angry
   Ⓒ anxious
   Ⓓ unchanged

Find an ANTONYM for each bold word. Then fill in the circle next to your answer.

7. Jaime has a **compassionate** nature.

   Ⓐ unsympathetic
   Ⓑ compatible
   Ⓒ patient
   Ⓓ meticulous

8. We could see his **ample** figure in the doorway.

   Ⓐ short
   Ⓑ reassuring
   Ⓒ skinny
   Ⓓ threatening

9. The performance **resumed** at 7:30 P.M.

   Ⓐ continued
   Ⓑ escalated
   Ⓒ deteriorated
   Ⓓ paused

10. The sounds of **mirth** filled the dance hall.

    Ⓐ mischief
    Ⓑ weeping
    Ⓒ jubilation
    Ⓓ relief

11. Camping always requires a great deal of **exertion.**

    Ⓐ foolhardiness
    Ⓑ carelessness
    Ⓒ knowledge
    Ⓓ relaxation

12. Caring for three dogs became a **burden** to Mr. Schmidt.

    Ⓐ problem
    Ⓑ failure
    Ⓒ help
    Ⓓ disaster

Choose the best way to complete each sentence or answer each question. Then fill in the circle next to your answer.

13. Because the trunk was **cumbersome,** I

    Ⓐ couldn't wait to open it.
    Ⓑ put a new coat of paint on it.
    Ⓒ put it in the kitchen.
    Ⓓ needed help carrying it.

14. A **jest** is

    Ⓐ an airplane.
    Ⓑ a stream of water.
    Ⓒ an insult.
    Ⓓ a joke.

15. Which of the following is a **moral** issue?

Ⓐ deciding what to eat for lunch
Ⓑ deciding whether to play basketball or handball
Ⓒ deciding whether to cheat on an exam
Ⓓ deciding when to go to bed

16. The package Hiroko was carrying was quite a **burden.** What was most likely to be inside?

Ⓐ a bag of carrots
Ⓑ four large books
Ⓒ a magazine
Ⓓ a letter

17. The **encounter** at Bunker Hill was costly for both sides. **Encounter** means

Ⓐ battle.
Ⓑ reunion.
Ⓒ feast.
Ⓓ mistake.

18. Brandon's **indignation** was caused by

Ⓐ finishing his report ahead of time.
Ⓑ bending over for too long.
Ⓒ hearing Aaron insult him.
Ⓓ working in the sun without a shirt.

19. After intermission, Sela **resumed** her place in the back row. This means that

Ⓐ she offered it to an elderly woman.
Ⓑ she moved to an empty seat in the front row.
Ⓒ she took someone else's seat.
Ⓓ she sat in the same place she was sitting before.

20. How might you react to a **ridiculous** idea?

Ⓐ by discussing it
Ⓑ by laughing at it
Ⓒ by supporting it
Ⓓ by frowning

21. Haley was **distressed** to learn that

Ⓐ there would be an exam tomorrow morning.
Ⓑ she didn't have to do the dishes.
Ⓒ she'd been accepted to play in the band.
Ⓓ her experiment had worked.

22. An **ample** supply of food will

Ⓐ run out quickly.
Ⓑ feed only a few people.
Ⓒ provide more than enough for everyone.
Ⓓ be acceptable to vegetarians.

23. **Compassion** for the stray animals caused Larisa to

Ⓐ forget about them.
Ⓑ complain about them.
Ⓒ joke about them.
Ⓓ give them shelter.

24. Maria was surprised to encounter an elephant on Main Street. This means that

Ⓐ Maria did not expect to see an elephant.
Ⓑ elephants often walk down Main Street.
Ⓒ the circus was in town.
Ⓓ Maria saw a poster of an elephant.

25. Madison didn't want to **exert** herself, so she

Ⓐ spent the day doing work in the yard.
Ⓑ taught her cousin to swim.
Ⓒ repaired the leaky sink.
Ⓓ took a long nap in the shade.

26. Which of the following could be a **moral** duty?

Ⓐ brushing your teeth
Ⓑ preserving the environment
Ⓒ doing your homework
Ⓓ e-mailing your friend

27. Sergio lives on the **outskirts** of St. Petersburg. Sergio lives

Ⓐ in the next town over.
Ⓑ at the foot of a mountain.
Ⓒ away from the center of St. Petersburg.
Ⓓ in the center of St. Petersburg.

28. Which would be considered **ridicule** of an elected official?

Ⓐ visiting a statue of him
Ⓑ making his ideas sound foolish
Ⓒ debating his ideas
Ⓓ reciting his speeches at public events

29. To **burden** a friend with a problem is to

Ⓐ work with her to solve it.
Ⓑ challenge her to solve it.
Ⓒ add your problem to her problems.
Ⓓ give her advice.

30. The horse **encountered** a stone wall. **Encountered** means

Ⓐ came to.
Ⓑ jumped over.
Ⓒ circled.
Ⓓ threw itself against.

31. Rachel was only **jesting** when she said she'd paint the house purple. **Jesting** means

Ⓐ thinking aloud.
Ⓑ planning ahead.
Ⓒ joking.
Ⓓ lying down.

Name ________________________________ Date ______________

Final Test 1

Read the passage. Choose the best answer for each sentence or question about a bold word. Then fill in the circle next to your answer.

The Tempest

The main **character** in Shakespeare's play *The Tempest* is Prospero, who was once the Duke of Milan. With the aid of King Alonso, Prospero's brother **overthrew** Prospero and made himself Duke. He then sent Prospero and his daughter, Miranda, out to sea in an old boat. Fortunately, Prospero and Miranda found **refuge** on an island. While Miranda was growing up, Prospero became an **accomplished** magician and **employed** spirits to do his bidding.

The play begins on a ship during a **tempest.** On board are Prospero's enemies—his brother Sebastian and King Alonso—along with King Alonso's son Ferdinand. When the ship is wrecked, the crew and passengers are all washed ashore.

King Alonso fears that his son Ferdinand has **perished.** However, Ferdinand has landed alone on another part of the island. There Ferdinand **encounters** Miranda and falls in love with her. Miranda takes Ferdinand to her father.

As Alonso and Sebastian search for Ferdinand, they become very hungry. They are frightened by a magical **banquet** that appears and then disappears. Becoming **visible** to them, the spirit Ariel tells them that they deserve to be punished for their earlier crimes. They begin to regret what they have done to Prospero and his daughter.

The play ends when all of the characters come face to face. Alonso is overjoyed to see his son alive but ashamed that he has discovered what he'd done in the past. It is agreed that Ferdinand and Miranda will marry and that all earlier wrongs will be **pardoned** and made right. Prospero once again becomes Duke of Milan. He **vows** to give up his magic and he sets his magical spirits free.

1. What does **character** mean in this passage?

   Ⓐ a person in a story
   Ⓑ the qualities that make up a person
   Ⓒ a symbol used in printing
   Ⓓ a ridiculous person

2. In this passage, **overthrew** means

   Ⓐ threw past the target.
   Ⓑ threw overboard.
   Ⓒ ended someone's rule.
   Ⓓ rejected a sweetheart.

3. When they found **refuge** on the island, they found

   Ⓐ shelter from bad weather.
   Ⓑ a safe place to live.
   Ⓒ another runaway.
   Ⓓ spirits living there.

4. Prospero was an **accomplished** magician. A SYNONYM for **accomplished** is

   Ⓐ well-known.
   Ⓑ substantial.
   Ⓒ assumed.
   Ⓓ expert.

5. In this passage, **employed** means

   Ⓐ enslaved.
   Ⓑ brought in.
   Ⓒ paid a wage to.
   Ⓓ used.

6. A **tempest** is

   Ⓐ a ship that is sinking.
   Ⓑ a riot.
   Ⓒ a wild storm with wind and rain.
   Ⓓ a blizzard.

7. Read this sentence from the passage.

   King Alonso fears that his son Ferdinand has perished.

   What is an ANTONYM for **perished?**

   Ⓐ survived
   Ⓑ drowned
   Ⓒ complied
   Ⓓ despaired

8. Read this sentence from the passage.

   There Ferdinand encounters Miranda and falls in love with her.

   What does **encounters** mean in this passage?

   Ⓐ introduces himself
   Ⓑ meets unexpectedly
   Ⓒ pledges himself to
   Ⓓ holds a long conversation with

9. Read these words from the passage.

   . . . a magical banquet that appears and then disappears.

   What does **banquet** mean in this passage?

   Ⓐ a bunch of flowers
   Ⓑ a frightening spirit
   Ⓒ a feast
   Ⓓ a small band of musicians

10. Read this sentence from the passage.

    Becoming* visible *to them, the spirit Ariel tells them that they deserve to be punished for their earlier crimes.

    Before Ariel becomes **visible** to the men, they

    Ⓐ argue with him.

    Ⓑ are scared by his monstrous appearance.

    Ⓒ are unable to see him.

    Ⓓ run from him.

11. Read these words from the passage.

    . . . all earlier wrongs will be* pardoned *. . .

    In this passage, **pardoned** means

    Ⓐ set free from jail.

    Ⓑ set free from slavery.

    Ⓒ punished.

    Ⓓ forgiven.

12. Read these words from the passage.

    He* vows *to give up his magic . . .

    What is a SYNONYM for **vow?**

    Ⓐ promise

    Ⓑ agree

    Ⓒ refuse

    Ⓓ hesitate

Name ______________________ Date ____________

Lessons 1–20

Final Test 2

Read the passage. Choose the best answer for each sentence or question about a bold word. Then fill in the circle next to your answer.

Petrified Forest National Park

In northeastern Arizona, the Petrified Forest National Park includes six forests of "stone trees." This is one of the world's largest and most colorful displays of **petrified** wood. The park covers over 218,533 acres. It consists of six separate "forests" that took over 200 million years to form. Long ago, this area was a flood plain where groves of tall trees **dominated** the land. The giant trees died naturally. Then they **toppled** and rolled down slight slopes into shallow swamps. There they formed **dense** logjams. Before the logs could deteriorate, they became waterlogged and sank into the swamps.

Flood waters and streams **proceeded** to flow into the swamps. These waters brought minerals and ashes from nearby volcanic **eruptions.** About four hundred feet of sandy mud covered the logs. This mud later turned into sandstone and shale.

Far below, the logs were undergoing a mysterious **transformation.** Minerals, mostly quartz, were **penetrating** the logs. The minerals replaced the cells made of vegetable matter. As the logs petrified, they **retained** their original shapes.

For millions of years the logs were **concealed** under layers of sandstone. Over time, **erosion** wore away the soft sandstone but not the hard quartz logs. Today these stone forests draw thousands of visitors a year to this desert area. The visitors are **fascinated** by the variety of colors of quartz seen there—red, brown, green, yellow, blue, and purple. If you decide to visit the site, you may hear a park ranger or tour guide refer to the petrified trees as the Rainbow Forest.

1. The logs **petrified** in the swamp. The logs

   Ⓐ became frightening to look at.
   Ⓑ turned to stone.
   Ⓒ sank deeper.
   Ⓓ slowly fell apart.

2. In this passage, **dominated** means

   Ⓐ clouded.
   Ⓑ rose high above.
   Ⓒ had an important position.
   Ⓓ reigned over.

3. What does **toppled** mean in this passage?

   Ⓐ rotted
   Ⓑ lost their powers
   Ⓒ fell over
   Ⓓ catapulted

4. A **dense** logjam is

   Ⓐ tightly packed.
   Ⓑ hard to see through.
   Ⓒ increasing.
   Ⓓ immense.

5. What does **proceeded** mean in this passage?

   Ⓐ went in front of
   Ⓑ happened before
   Ⓒ were forced
   Ⓓ went on

6. In this passage, **eruptions** are

Ⓐ outbursts of anger.
Ⓑ bursts of molten rock.
Ⓒ visible volcanoes.
Ⓓ poisonous fumes.

7. A SYNONYM for **transformation** is

Ⓐ combination.
Ⓑ movement.
Ⓒ change.
Ⓓ excavation.

8. What does **penetrating** mean in this passage?

Ⓐ stabbing
Ⓑ piercing
Ⓒ investigating
Ⓓ passing into

9. Read these words from the passage.

. . . they retained their original shapes . . .

What is an ANTONYM for **retained?**

Ⓐ lost
Ⓑ kept
Ⓒ established
Ⓓ preserved

10. Read this sentence from the passage.

*For millions of years the logs were **concealed** under layers of sandstone.*

In this passage, **concealed** means

Ⓐ weighted down.
Ⓑ forgotten.
Ⓒ hidden.
Ⓓ put away in a safe place.

11. According to this passage, what happened during the process of **erosion?**

    Ⓐ The trees began turning to stone.
    Ⓑ Wind and rain wore away the soft sandstone.
    Ⓒ The quartz turned into different colors.
    Ⓓ The logs were dug up by park rangers.

12. Read these words from the passage.

    The visitors are **fascinated** ***by the variety of colors . . .***

    This means that

    Ⓐ the visitors feel small in the forest.
    Ⓑ the visitors are illuminated by the forest.
    Ⓒ the visitors are made nostalgic by the forest.
    Ⓓ the forest holds the visitors' attention and interest.

Name ______________________ Date ____________

Final Test 3

Read the passage. Choose the best answer for each sentence or question about a bold word. Then fill in the circle next to your answer.

The Remarkable Nellie Bly

Elizabeth Cochran was born into a large **prosperous** family in 1864. However, her father died when she was six, and the family fortunes declined. At fifteen, she started teachers' college but had to drop out for lack of money. It seemed unjust that her poorly educated brothers landed jobs as clerks but jobs for women were mostly **restricted** to work as servants and factory hands.

For five years she helped her mother run a boarding house. One day she read an upsetting article in the *Pittsburgh Dispatch*. It was written by a man who looked at the past with a great deal of **nostalgia.** He stated that women belonged in the home and that it was **monstrous** for a woman to try to make a living outside of it. Elizabeth was so **indignant** that she wrote a long letter to the editor pointing out that many women had no choice but to work for a living. Impressed by her spirit, the editor asked her to see him.

He offered her a job, and she took the pen name Nellie Bly. At first, she was able to write the stories that she wanted. She tried to bring **moral** issues—poverty, child labor, and the poor treatment of factory girls—to the public's attention. When she was asked to work on the women's pages, she went to Mexico instead and sent back stories that reflected her **aggressive** attitude toward getting news.

Back home, she went to see the editor of the *New York World*. She proposed a story to him: she would **investigate** conditions in an institution for mad people—from the inside. She **assumed** madness and was easily admitted to an institution. After several days, she tried to **convince** the doctors that she was sane, but they refused to believe her. Once the newspaper's lawyer got her released, she wrote a shocking story about the staff's cruelty.

All her life, Nellie continued to do things and write stories that amazed the public. She was among the most **brilliant** and well-known newspaper writers of her time. She died in 1922, on the same day that one of her closest friends died—the man who had written the same **exasperating** article about women belonging in the home.

1. What does **prosperous** mean in this passage?

   Ⓐ respected
   Ⓑ wealthy
   Ⓒ well-known
   Ⓓ celebrated

2. A SYNONYM for **restricted** is

   Ⓐ given.
   Ⓑ reserved.
   Ⓒ limited.
   Ⓓ dedicated.

3. **Nostalgia** is the feeling that

   Ⓐ the past was a better time.
   Ⓑ the past is better forgotten.
   Ⓒ the world is always getting better.
   Ⓓ women should be homemakers.

4. In this passage, **monstrous** means

   Ⓐ huge.
   Ⓑ shocking.
   Ⓒ deformed.
   Ⓓ frightening.

5. What does **indignant** mean?

   Ⓐ angry about something unfair
   Ⓑ cold and indifferent
   Ⓒ better informed
   Ⓓ miserable

6. Nelly Bly addressed **moral** issues in her newspaper articles. These articles had to do with

Ⓐ recipes and cooking.
Ⓑ her family.
Ⓒ questions of right and wrong.
Ⓓ secrets and gossip.

7. Nelly Bly was an **aggressive** reporter. In this passage, **aggressive** means

Ⓐ fierce.
Ⓑ bold.
Ⓒ beginning.
Ⓓ uneducated.

8. To **investigate** conditions is to

Ⓐ look into them closely.
Ⓑ wish they were better.
Ⓒ do nothing about them.
Ⓓ make improvements to them.

9. How did Nelly Bly **assume** madness?

Ⓐ She understood madness.
Ⓑ She took madness for granted.
Ⓒ She pretended to be mad.
Ⓓ She pretended to be a doctor.

10. A SYNONYM for **convince** is

Ⓐ propose.
Ⓑ persuade.
Ⓒ alert.
Ⓓ proclaim.

11. In this passage, **brilliant** means

    Ⓐ shining.
    Ⓑ heroic.
    Ⓒ under appreciated.
    Ⓓ clever.

12. The **exasperating** article in this passage caused Nelly Bly to feel

    Ⓐ annoyed.
    Ⓑ hilarious.
    Ⓒ ridiculous.
    Ⓓ foolhardy.

Name ______________________________ Date ______________

Final Test 4

Read the passage. Choose the best answer for each sentence or question about a bold word. Then fill in the circle next to your answer.

Very Grim Fairy Tales

Folk tales and fairy tales are often considered children's entertainment. You are probably familiar with such stories as Cinderella and Rumplestiltskin. As originally told, these folk tales were different from the stories that you know. Many of our long-ago **ancestors** told these stories not only to entertain their friends and families, but also to **establish** guidelines for proper behavior.

In 1806, two brothers named Jacob and Wilhelm Grimm were inspired to start collecting and **preserving** the stories of their homeland. Very **methodically,** they collected and recorded more than 200 tales. Today we know this collection as *Grimm's Fairy Tales.*

The original stories bear a general **likeness** to the versions you probably know. The most **significant** characters have some sort of hardship, poverty, or **disaster** to overcome. They are certain to overcome their **afflictions,** however, because they are kind-hearted, clever, and hardworking. And in the end, they do. They become wealthy, notable, or they **liberate** their loved ones from horrible spells or villains.

The losers are **foolhardy** and greedy. In both the older and newer versions, the wicked live unhappily ever after. But the original tales were much more **grim.** In **painstaking** detail, the storytellers described the horrible punishments inflicted on the wicked. The lesson of the story and the price of ignoring it could not be easily forgotten.

1. Which of the following could be your **ancestors?**

   Ⓐ your closest friends
   Ⓑ your teachers
   Ⓒ your children and grandchildren
   Ⓓ your grandparents and great-grandparents

2. In this passage, **establish** means

   Ⓐ prove.
   Ⓑ found.
   Ⓒ set up.
   Ⓓ remove.

3. What did the brothers Grimm do to **preserve** the stories of their homeland?

   Ⓐ They collected and recorded them.
   Ⓑ They read them aloud.
   Ⓒ They gave them away.
   Ⓓ They made movies out of them.

4. The Grimms were **methodical** about their task. What does this mean?

   Ⓐ They did not want to complete their task.
   Ⓑ They did not tell anyone about their task.
   Ⓒ They would not allow anyone to help with their task.
   Ⓓ They were careful and orderly with their task.

5. In this passage, **likeness** means

   Ⓐ similarity.
   Ⓑ portrait.
   Ⓒ photograph.
   Ⓓ difference.

6. What are the most **significant** characters?

   Ⓐ the characters that appear most often
   Ⓑ the oldest characters
   Ⓒ the most important characters
   Ⓓ the most wicked characters

7. What does **disaster** mean in this passage?

   Ⓐ a brief meeting
   Ⓑ a great misfortune
   Ⓒ a slight illness
   Ⓓ a foreign language

8. The story characters must overcome their **afflictions.** A SYNONYM for **affliction** is

   Ⓐ suffering.
   Ⓑ fear.
   Ⓒ nervousness.
   Ⓓ tiredness.

9. Some characters **liberate** their loved ones from spells. What is a SYNONYM for **liberate?**

   Ⓐ lose
   Ⓑ transform
   Ⓒ teach
   Ⓓ free

10. An ANTONYM for **foolhardy** is

    Ⓐ mischievous.
    Ⓑ hilarious.
    Ⓒ wise.
    Ⓓ strong.

11. According to the passage, the original tales were more **grim.** This means that the original tales were more

    Ⓐ interesting.
    Ⓑ frivolous.
    Ⓒ true.
    Ⓓ disturbing.

12. **Painstaking** details

    Ⓐ are not important.
    Ⓑ show great effort.
    Ⓒ are easy to collect.
    Ⓓ are hurtful to read.

Answer Key

Lesson 1

1. C
2. B
3. D
4. A
5. C
6. B
7. A
8. C
9. C
10. D
11. A
12. C
13. A
14. A
15. B
16. C
17. C
18. A
19. B
20. D
21. C
22. A
23. B
24. A
25. B
26. C
27. D

Lesson 2

1. C
2. B
3. D
4. C
5. B
6. A
7. B
8. B
9. A
10. D
11. B
12. C
13. A
14. D
15. C
16. D
17. B
18. C
19. B
20. A
21. C
22. A
23. D
24. C
25. A
26. B
27. A
28. C
29. C
30. B
31. B
32. C
33. C
34. C

Lesson 3

1. A
2. C
3. B
4. C
5. D
6. B
7. A
8. C
9. A
10. D
11. C
12. B
13. B
14. A
15. D
16. C
17. C
18. B
19. A
20. C
21. B
22. C
23. D
24. D
25. C
26. B
27. A
28. C
29. C
30. D

Lesson 4

1. C
2. B
3. A
4. B
5. A
6. D
7. C
8. A
9. B
10. D
11. C
12. C
13. B
14. A
15. B
16. C
17. D
18. B
19. C
20. A
21. D
22. A
23. C
24. D
25. A
26. B
27. C
28. D
29. C

Lesson 5

1. C
2. B
3. D
4. B
5. C
6. D
7. B
8. C
9. A
10. C
11. D
12. C
13. B
14. A
15. B
16. C
17. C
18. D
19. B
20. A
21. D
22. D
23. A
24. B
25. A
26. C
27. D
28. B
29. A

Lesson 6

1. A
2. D
3. C
4. B
5. B
6. C
7. A
8. D
9. B
10. D
11. A
12. C
13. D
14. C
15. A
16. B
17. C
18. D
19. B
20. C
21. C
22. D
23. A
24. A
25. C
26. D
27. B
28. C

Lesson 7

1. D
2. B
3. D
4. A
5. D
6. B
7. A
8. A
9. B
10. C
11. D
12. B
13. C
14. C
15. D
16. A
17. A
18. B
19. D
20. B
21. C
22. A
23. D
24. C

Answer Key

25. B
26. D
27. C
28. A
29. C
30. B
31. A
32. D
33. A
34. D
35. C
36. B

Lesson 8

1. C
2. B
3. A
4. D
5. D
6. C
7. B
8. A
9. C
10. D
11. C
12. B
13. A
14. C
15. D
16. B
17. B
18. C
19. B
20. B
21. B
22. C
23. A
24. D
25. B
26. C
27. B
28. C
29. A

Lesson 9

1. C
2. B
3. D
4. C
5. A
6. B
7. C
8. C
9. B
10. A
11. B
12. D
13. C
14. D
15. C
16. B
17. A
18. A
19. C
20. C
21. D
22. A
23. C
24. A
25. B
26. B
27. D
28. C
29. C

Lesson 10

1. B
2. D
3. C
4. C
5. A
6. D
7. B
8. A
9. B
10. C
11. D
12. A
13. A
14. B
15. C
16. D
17. C
18. B
19. B
20. D
21. A
22. B
23. A
24. C
25. A
26. B
27. B
28. D
29. C
30. C
31. C

Midterm Test 1 (Lessons 1–10)

1. B
2. C
3. A
4. D
5. C
6. B
7. D
8. A
9. C
10. B
11. A
12. D

Midterm Test 2 (Lessons 1–10)

1. D
2. C
3. D
4. B
5. C
6. D
7. A
8. A
9. C
10. B
11. A
12. B

Lesson 11

1. D
2. B
3. A
4. C
5. D
6. B
7. A
8. C
9. D
10. C
11. C
12. B
13. A
14. C
15. D
16. B
17. D
18. A
19. B
20. B
21. C
22. B
23. D
24. A
25. C
26. D
27. B
28. C
29. D
30. D
31. A
32. B
33. C

Lesson 12

1. B
2. A
3. C
4. D
5. B
6. C
7. D
8. B
9. A
10. C
11. B
12. D
13. C
14. B
15. B
16. C
17. A
18. C
19. B
20. C
21. C
22. D
23. A
24. B
25. D
26. C
27. D
28. D
29. B

Lesson 13

1. A
2. C
3. B
4. D
5. B
6. D
7. C
8. A
9. B
10. D
11. C
12. C

Answer Key

13. B
14. A
15. D
16. C
17. D
18. C
19. B
20. B
21. A
22. C
23. D
24. B
25. C

Lesson 14

1. B
2. B
3. A
4. C
5. D
6. C
7. B
8. A
9. D
10. D
11. C
12. D
13. C
14. B
15. A
16. C
17. C
18. B
19. A
20. C
21. B
22. C
23. D
24. A
25. B
26. B
27. D
28. C
29. B
30. A
31. D
32. B

Lesson 15

1. C
2. B
3. C
4. D
5. B
6. C
7. D
8. A
9. B
10. D
11. A
12. A
13. B
14. B
15. D
16. C
17. A
18. C
19. B
20. C
21. C
22. D
23. C
24. B
25. C
26. C
27. A
28. D
29. B
30. C
31. A

Lesson 16

1. B
2. C
3. D
4. A
5. D
6. D
7. B
8. A
9. B
10. A
11. D
12. C
13. A
14. D
15. D
16. D
17. C
18. B
19. B
20. A
21. C
22. D
23. C
24. C
25. D
26. C
27. B
28. A
29. B
30. C
31. D

Lesson 17

1. B
2. A
3. C
4. D
5. C
6. D
7. B
8. D
9. D
10. C
11. C
12. C
13. B
14. C
15. B
16. C
17. A
18. A
19. B
20. C
21. A
22. C
23. B
24. C
25. D
26. C

Lesson 18

1. C
2. C
3. A
4. D
5. B
6. B
7. D
8. C
9. C
10. A
11. B
12. D
13. B
14. A
15. B
16. C
17. D
18. C
19. C
20. D
21. D
22. B
23. C
24. D
25. B
26. C
27. A
28. B
29. A
30. C
31. D

Lesson 19

1. C
2. C
3. A
4. D
5. B
6. A
7. B
8. B
9. C
10. B
11. C
12. B
13. D
14. A
15. B
16. A
17. C
18. C
19. D
20. C
21. B
22. C
23. D
24. B
25. A
26. C

Answer Key

Lesson 20

1. C
2. B
3. A
4. C
5. D
6. B
7. A
8. C
9. D
10. B
11. D
12. C
13. D
14. D
15. C
16. B
17. A
18. C
19. D
20. B
21. A
22. C
23. D
24. A
25. D
26. B
27. C
28. B
29. C
30. A
31. C

Final Test 1 (Lessons 1–20)

1. A
2. C
3. B
4. D
5. D
6. C
7. A
8. B
9. C
10. C
11. D
12. A

Final Test 2 (Lessons 1–20)

1. B
2. B
3. C
4. A
5. D
6. B
7. C
8. B
9. A
10. C
11. B
12. D

Final Test 3 (Lessons 1–20)

1. B
2. C
3. A
4. B
5. A
6. C
7. B
8. A
9. C
10. B
11. D
12. A

Final Test 4 (Lessons 1–20)

1. D
2. C
3. A
4. D
5. A
6. C
7. B
8. A
9. D
10. C
11. D
12. B